KU-711-909

Praise for

The Art of Thinking Clearly

'No wonder this book has been a sensation in Europe. Dobelli examines our most common decision-making failings with engaging eloquence and describes how to counter them with instructive good sense.'
Robert Cialdini

'This book will change the way you think.'
Dan Goldstein, London Business School

'This book provides a truly fresh perspective. It is intelligent, informative and witty. Rolf Dobelli's clear prose illuminates how we think.'
Christoph Franz, Global CEO, Lufthansa Airlines

'A treat – highly relevant, scientifically grounded and beautifully written.'
Claudio Feser, CEO McKinsey, Switzerland

'A fireworks show of insights into how our minds work.'
Iris Bohnet, Harvard Kennedy School

For Sabine

The Art of Thinking Clearly

ROLF DOBELLI

TRANSLATED BY NICKY GRIFFIN

SCEPTRE

First published in Great Britain in 2013 by Sceptre
An imprint of Hodder & Stoughton
An Hachette UK company

First published in paperback in 2014

2

A CIP catalogue record for this title is available from the British Library

B format paperback ISBN 978 1 444 75956 3
A format paperback ISBN 978 1 444 79487 8
eBook ISBN 978 1 444 75955 6

Printed and bound by Clays Ltd, St Ives plc

Hodder & Stoughton policy is to use papers that are natural, renewable
and recyclable products and made from wood grown in sustainable
forests. The logging and manufacturing processes are expected to
conform to the environmental regulations of the country of origin.

Hodder & Stoughton Ltd
338 Euston Road
London NW1 3BH

www.sceptrebooks.co.uk

CONTENTS

CONTENTS

INTRODUCTION

In the fall of 2004, a European media mogul invited me to Munich to partake in what was described as an 'informal exchange of intellectuals'. I had never considered myself an 'intellectual' – I had studied business, which made me quite the opposite, really – but I had also written two literary novels and that, I guessed, must have qualified me for such an invitation.

Nassim Nicholas Taleb was sitting at the table. At that time, he was an obscure Wall Street trader with a penchant for philosophy. I was introduced to him as an authority on the English and Scottish Enlightenment, particularly the philosophy of David Hume. Obviously I had been mixed up with someone else. Stunned, I nevertheless flashed a hesitant smile around the room and let the resulting silence act as proof of my philosophical prowess. Straight away, Taleb pulled over a free chair and patted the seat. I sat down. After a cursory exchange about Hume, the conversation mercifully shifted to Wall Street. We marveled at the systematic errors in decision making that CEOs and business leaders make – ourselves included. We chatted about the fact that unexpected events seem much more likely in retrospect. We chuckled about why it is that investors cannot part with their shares when they drop below acquisition price.

Following the event, Taleb sent me pages from his manuscript, a gem of a book, which I commented on and partly criticised. These went on to form part of his international best-seller, *The Black Swan*. The book catapulted Taleb into the intellectual all-star league. Meanwhile, my appetite whetted, I began to devour books and articles written by cognitive and social scientists on topics such as 'heuristics and biases', and I also increased my email conversations with a large number of researchers and started to visit their labs. By 2009, I had realised that, alongside my job as a novelist, I had become a student of social and cognitive psychology.

The failure to think clearly, or what experts call a 'cognitive error', is a systematic deviation from logic – from optimal, rational, reasonable thought and behaviour. By 'systematic' I mean that these are not just occasional errors in judgement, but rather routine mistakes, barriers to logic we stumble over time and again, repeating patterns through generations and through the centuries. For example, it is much more common that we overestimate our knowledge than that we underestimate it. Similarly, the danger of losing something stimulates us much more than the prospect of making a similar gain. In the presence of other people we tend to adjust our behaviour to theirs, not the opposite. Anecdotes make us overlook the statistical distribution (base rate) behind it, not the other way round. The errors we make follow the same pattern over and over again, piling up in one specific, predictable corner like dirty laundry while the other corner remains relatively clean (i.e. they pile up in the 'overconfidence corner', not the 'underconfidence corner').

To avoid frivolous gambles with the wealth I had accumulated over the course of my literary career, I began to put together a list of these systematic cognitive errors, complete with notes and personal anecdotes – with no intention of ever publishing them. The list was originally designed to be used by me alone. Some of these thinking errors have been known for centuries; others have been discovered in the last few years. Some come with two or three names attached to them. I chose the terms most widely used. Soon I realised that such a compilation of pitfalls was not only useful for making investing decisions, but also for business and personal matters. Once I had prepared the list, I felt calmer and more clearheaded. I began to recognise my own errors sooner and was able to change course before any lasting damage was done. And, for the first time in my life, I was able to recognise when others might be in thrall to these very same systematic errors. Armed with my list, I could now resist their pull – and perhaps even gain an upper hand in my dealings. I now had categories, terms, and explanations with which to ward off the spectre of irrationality. Since Benjamin Franklin's kite-flying days, thunder and lightning have not grown less frequent, powerful or loud – but they have become less worrisome. This is exactly how I feel about my own irrationality now.

Friends soon learned of my compendium and showed interest. This led to a weekly newspaper column in Germany, Holland and Switzerland, countless presentations (mostly to medical doctors, investors, board members, CEOs and government officials) and eventually to this book.

Please keep in mind three things as you peruse these pages: first, the list of fallacies in this book is not complete. Undoubtedly new ones will be discovered. Second, the majority of these errors are related to one another. This should come as no surprise. After all, all brain regions are linked. Neural projections travel from region to region in the brain; no area functions independently. Third, I am primarily a novelist and an entrepreneur, not a social scientist; I don't have my own lab where I can conduct experiments on cognitive errors, nor do I have a staff of researchers I can dispatch to scout for behavioural errors. In writing this book, I think of myself as a translator whose job is to interpret and synthesise what I've read and learned – to put it in terms others can understand. My great respect goes to the researchers who, in recent decades, have uncovered these behavioural and cognitive errors. The success of this book is fundamentally a tribute to their research. I am enormously indebted to them.

This is not a how-to book. You won't find 'seven steps to an error-free life' here. Cognitive errors are far too ingrained for us to be able to rid ourselves of them completely. Silencing them would require superhuman willpower, but that isn't even a worthy goal. Not all cognitive errors are toxic, and some are even necessary for leading a good life. Although this book may not hold the key to happiness, at the very least it acts as insurance against too much self-induced unhappiness.

Indeed, my wish is quite simple: if we could learn to recognise and evade the biggest errors in thinking – in our private lives, at work or in government – we might experience a leap in prosperity. We need no extra cunning, no new ideas, no unnecessary gadgets, no frantic hyperactivity – all we need is less irrationality.

1

WHY YOU SHOULD VISIT CEMETERIES

Survivorship Bias

No matter where Rick looks, he sees rock stars. They appear on television, on the front pages of magazines, in concert programmes and at online fan sites. Their songs are unavoidable – in the mall, on his playlist, in the gym. The rock stars are everywhere. There are lots of them. And they are successful. Motivated by the stories of countless guitar heroes, Rick starts a band. Will he make it big? The probability lies a fraction above zero. Like so many others, he will most likely end up in the graveyard of failed musicians. This burial ground houses 10,000 times more musicians than the stage does, but no journalist is interested in failures – with the exception of fallen superstars. This makes the cemetery invisible to outsiders.

In daily life, because triumph is made more visible than failure, you systematically overestimate your chances of succeeding. As an outsider, you (like Rick) succumb to an illusion, and you mistake how minuscule the probability of success really is. Rick, like so many others, is a victim of *Survivorship Bias*.

Behind every popular author you can find 100 other writers whose books will never sell. Behind them are another 100 who haven't found publishers. Behind them are yet another

100 whose unfinished manuscripts gather dust in drawers. And behind each one of these are 100 people who dream of – one day – writing a book. You, however, hear of only the successful authors (these days, many of them self-published) and fail to recognise how unlikely literary success is. The same goes for photographers, entrepreneurs, artists, athletes, architects, Nobel Prize winners, television presenters and beauty queens. The media is not interested in digging around in the graveyards of the unsuccessful. Nor is this its job. To elude the *survivorship bias*, you must do the digging yourself.

You will also come across *survivorship bias* when dealing with money and risk: imagine that a friend founds a start-up. You belong to the circle of potential investors and you sense a real opportunity: this could be the next Google. Maybe you'll be lucky. But what is the reality? The most likely scenario is that the company will not even make it off the starting line. The second most likely outcome is that it will go bankrupt within three years. Of the companies that survive these first three years, most never grow to more than ten employees. So, should you never put your hard-earned money at risk? Not necessarily. But you should recognise that the *survivorship bias* is at work, distorting the probability of success like cut glass.

Take the Dow Jones Industrial Average Index. It consists of out-and-out survivors. Failed and small businesses do not enter the stock market, and yet these represent the majority of business ventures. A stock index is not indicative of a country's economy. Similarly, the press does not report proportionately on all musicians. The vast number of books and coaches dealing with success should also make you sceptical: the unsuccessful don't write books or give lectures on their failures.

Survivorship bias can become especially pernicious when you become a member of the 'winning' team. Even if your success stems from pure coincidence, you'll discover similarities with other winners and be tempted to mark these as 'success factors'. However, if you ever visit the graveyard of failed individuals and companies, you will realise that its tenants possessed many of the same traits that characterise your success.

If enough scientists examine a particular phenomenon, a few of these studies will deliver statistically significant results through pure coincidence – for example the relationship between red wine consumption and high life expectancy. Such (false) studies immediately attain a high degree of popularity and attention. As a result, you will not read about the studies with the 'boring', but correct results.

Survivorship bias means this: people systematically overestimate their chances of success. Guard against it by frequently visiting the graves of once-promising projects, investments and careers. It is a sad walk, but one that should clear your mind.

See also **Self-serving Bias** (ch. 45); **Beginner's Luck** (ch. 49); **Base-Rate Neglect** (ch. 28); **Induction** (ch. 31); **Neglect of Probability** (ch. 26); **Illusion of Skill** (ch. 94); **Intention-To-Treat Error** (ch. 98)

2

DOES HARVARD MAKE YOU SMARTER?

Swimmer's Body Illusion

As essayist and trader Nassim Taleb resolved to do something about the stubborn extra pounds he'd be carrying, he contemplated taking up various sports. However, joggers seemed scrawny and unhappy, and bodybuilders looked broad and stupid, and cyclists? Oh, so bottom-heavy! Swimmers, though, appealed to him with their well-built, streamlined bodies. He decided to sign up at his local swimming pool and to train hard twice a week.

A short while later, he realised that he had succumbed to an illusion. Professional swimmers don't have perfect bodies because they train extensively. Rather, they are good swimmers because of their physiques. How their bodies are designed is a factor for selection and not the result of their activities. Similarly, female models advertise cosmetics and thus, many female consumers believe that these products make you beautiful. But it is not the cosmetics that make these women model-like. Quite simply, the models are born attractive and only for this reason are they candidates for cosmetics advertising. As with the swimmers' bodies, beauty is a factor for selection and not the result.

Whenever we confuse selection factors with results, we fall prey to what Taleb calls the *swimmer's body illusion*.

Without this illusion, half of advertising campaigns would not work. But this bias has to do with more than just the pursuit of chiselled cheekbones and chests. For example, Harvard has the reputation of being a top university. Many highly successful people have studied there. Does this mean that Harvard is a good school? We don't know. Perhaps the school is terrible, and it simply recruits the brightest students around. I experienced this phenomenon at the University of St Gallen in Switzerland. It is said to be one of the top ten business schools in Europe, but the lessons I received (although note that this was twenty-five years ago) were mediocre. Nevertheless, many of its graduates were successful. The reason behind this is unknown – perhaps it was due to the climate in the narrow valley or even the cafeteria food. Most probable, however, is the rigorous selection.

All over the world, MBA schools lure candidates with statistics regarding future income. This simple calculation is supposed to show that the horrendously high tuition fees pay for themselves after a short period of time. Many prospective students fall for this approach. I am not implying that the schools doctor the statistics, but still their statements must not be swallowed wholesale. Why? Because those who pursue an MBA are different from those who do not. The income gap between these groups stems from a multitude of reasons that have nothing to do with the MBA degree itself. Once again we see the *swimmer's body illusion* at work: the factor for selection confused with the result. So, if you are considering further study, do it for reasons other than a bigger pay cheque.

When I ask happy people about the secret of their contentment, I often hear answers like 'You have to see the glass half-full rather than half-empty.' It is as if these individuals do not realise that they were born happy, and now tend to see the positive in everything. They do not realise that cheerfulness – according to many studies, such as those conducted by Harvard's Dan Gilbert – is largely a personality trait that remains constant throughout life. Or, as social scientists Lykken and Tellegen starkly suggest, 'trying to be happier is as futile as trying to be taller.' Thus, the *swimmer's body illusion* is also a self-illusion. When these optimists write self-help books, the illusion can become treacherous. That's why it's important to give a wide berth to tips and advice from self-help authors. For billions of people, these pieces of advice are unlikely to help. But because the unhappy don't write self-help books about their failures, this fact remains hidden.

In conclusion: be wary when you are encouraged to strive for certain things – be it abs of steel, immaculate looks, a higher income, a long life, a particular demeanour or happiness. You might fall prey to the *swimmer's body illusion*. Before you decide to take the plunge, look in the mirror – and be honest about what you see.

See also **Halo Effect** (ch. 38); **Outcome Bias** (ch. 20); **Self-Selection Bias** (ch. 47); **Alternative Blindness** (ch. 71); **Fundamental Attribution Error** (ch. 36)

3

WHY YOU SEE SHAPES IN THE CLOUDS

Clustering Illusion

In 1957, Swedish opera singer Friedrich Jorgensen bought a tape player to record his vocals. When he listened back to the recording, he heard strange noises throughout, whispers that sounded like supernatural messages. A few years later, he recorded birdsong. This time, he heard the voice of his deceased mother in the background whispering to him: 'Fried, my little Fried, can you hear me? It's Mammy.' That did it. Jorgensen turned his life around and devoted himself to communicating with the deceased via tape recordings.

In 1994, Diane Duyser from Florida also had an otherworldly encounter. After biting into a slice of toast and placing it back down on the plate, she noticed the face of the Virgin Mary in it. Immediately, she stopped eating and stored the divine message (minus a bite) in a plastic container. In November 2004, she auctioned the still fairly well preserved snack on eBay. Her daily bread earned her $28,000.

In 1978, a woman from New Mexico had a similar experience. Her tortilla's blackened spots resembled Jesus' face. The press latched on to the story, and thousands of people flocked to New Mexico to see the saviour in burrito form. Two years earlier, in 1976, the orbiter of the Viking

Spacecraft had photographed a rock formation that, from high above, looked like a human face. The 'Face on Mars' made headlines around the world.

And you? Have you ever seen faces in the clouds or the outlines of animals in rocks? Of course. This is perfectly normal. The human brain seeks patterns and rules. In fact, it takes it one step further: if it finds no familiar patterns, it simply invents some. The more diffuse the signal, such as the background noise on the tape, the easier it is to find 'hidden messages' in it. Twenty-five years after uncovering the 'Face on Mars', the Mars Global Surveyor sent back crisp, clear images of the rock formations: the captivating human face had dissolved into plain old scree.

These frothy examples make the clustering illusion seem innocuous; it is not. Consider the financial markets, which churn out floods of data every second. Grinning ear to ear, a friend told me that he had discovered a pattern in the sea of data: 'If you multiply the percentage change of the Dow Jones by the percentage change of the oil price, you get the move of the gold price in two days' time.' In other words, if share prices and oil climb or fall in unison, gold will rise the day after tomorrow. His theory worked well for a few weeks, until he began to speculate with ever-larger sums and eventually squandered his savings. He had sensed a pattern where none existed.

oxxxoxxxoxxoooxooxxoo. Is this sequence random or planned? Psychology professor Thomas Gilovich interviewed hundreds of people for an answer. Most did not want to believe the sequence was arbitrary. They figured some law must govern the order of the letters. Wrong, explained Gilovich, and pointed to some dice: it is quite possible to roll the same number four times in a row, which mystifies many people. Apparently we have trouble accepting that such events can take place by chance.

During WWII, the Germans bombed London. Among other ammunition, they used V1 rockets, a kind of self-navigating drone. With each attack, the impact sites were carefully plotted on a map, terrifying Londoners: they thought they had discovered a pattern, and developed theories about which parts of the city were the safest. However, after the war, statistical analysis confirmed that the distribution was totally random. Today it's clear why: the V1's navigation system was extremely inaccurate.

In conclusion: when it comes to pattern recognition, we are oversensitive. Regain your scepticism. If you think you have discovered a pattern, first consider it pure chance. If it seems too good to be true, find a mathematician and have the data tested statistically. And if the crispy parts of your pancake start to look a lot like Jesus' face, ask yourself: if he really wants to reveal himself, why doesn't he do it in Times Square or on CNN?

See also **Illusion of Control** (ch. 17); **Coincidence** (ch. 24); **False Causality** (ch. 37)

4

IF 50 MILLION PEOPLE SAY SOMETHING FOOLISH, IT IS STILL FOOLISH

Social Proof

You are on your way to a concert. At an intersection, you encounter a group of people, all staring at the sky. Without even thinking about it, you peer upwards too. Why? *Social proof.* In the middle of the concert, when the soloist is displaying absolute mastery, someone begins to clap and suddenly the whole room joins in. You do, too. Why? *Social proof.* After the concert you go to the coat check to pick up your coat. You watch how the people in front of you place a coin on a plate, even though, officially, the service is included in the ticket price. What do you do? You probably leave a tip as well.

Social proof, sometimes roughly termed the *herd instinct,* dictates that individuals feel they are behaving correctly when they act the same as other people. In other words, the more people who follow a certain idea, the better (truer) we deem the idea to be. And the more people who display a certain behaviour the more appropriate this behaviour is judged to be by others. This is, of course, absurd.

Social proof is the evil behind bubbles and stock market panic. It exists in fashion, management techniques, hobbies, religion and diets. It can paralyse whole cultures, such as when sects commit collective suicide.

A simple experiment carried out in the 1950s by legendary psychologist Solomon Asch shows how peer pressure can warp common sense. A subject is shown a line drawn on paper, and next to it three lines – numbered 1, 2 and 3 – one shorter, one longer and one of the same length as the original one. He or she must indicate which of the three lines corresponds to the original one. If the person is alone in the room, he gives correct answers – unsurprising, because the task is really quite simple. Now five other people enter the room; they are all actors, which the subject does not know. One after another, they give wrong answers, saying 'number 1', although it's very clear that number 3 is the correct answer. Then it is the subject's turn again. In one third of cases, he will answer incorrectly to match the other people's responses.

Why do we act like this? Well, in the past, following others was a good survival strategy. Suppose that 50,000 years ago, you were travelling around the Serengeti with your hunter-gatherer friends, and suddenly they all bolted. What would you have done? Would you have stayed put, scratching your head, and weighing up whether what you were looking at was a lion or something that just looked like a lion but was in fact a harmless animal that could serve as a great protein source? No, you would have sprinted after your friends. Later on, when you were safe, you could have reflected on what the 'lion' had actually been. Those who acted differently from the group – and I am sure there were some – exited the gene pool. We are the direct descendants of those who copied the others' behaviour. This pattern is so deeply rooted in us that we still use it today, even when it offers no survival advantage, which is most of the time. Only a few cases come to mind where social proof is of value. For example, if you find yourself hungry in a foreign city and don't know a good restaurant, it makes sense to pick the one that's full of locals. In other words, you copy the locals' behaviour.

Comedy and talk shows make use of *social proof* by inserting canned laughter at strategic spots, inciting the audience to laugh along. One of the most impressive, though troubling, cases of this phenomenon is the famous speech by Nazi propaganda minister Joseph Goebbels, delivered to a large audience in 1943. (See it for yourself on YouTube.) As the war went from bad to worse for Germany, he demanded to know: 'Do you want total war? If necessary, do you want a war more total and radical than anything that we can even imagine today?' The crowd roared. If the attendees had been asked individually and anonymously, it is likely that nobody would have consented to this crazy proposal.

The advertising industry benefits greatly from our weakness for *social proof*. This works well when a situation is unclear (such as deciding among various car makes, cleaning products, beauty products etc. with no obvious advantages or disadvantages), and where people 'like you and me' appear.

So, be sceptical whenever a company claims its product is better because it is 'the most popular'. How is a product better simply because it sells the most units? And remember novelist W. Somerset Maugham's wise words: 'If 50 million people say something foolish, it is still foolish.'

See also **Groupthink** (ch. 25); **Social Loafing** (ch. 33); **In-Group Out-Group Bias** (ch. 79); **False-Consensus Effect** (ch. 77)

5

WHY YOU SHOULD FORGET THE PAST

Sunk Cost Fallacy

The film was dire. After an hour, I whispered to my wife: 'Come on, let's go home.' She replied: 'No way. We're not throwing away $30.' 'That's no reason to stay,' I protested. 'The money's already gone. This is the *sunk cost fallacy* at work – a thinking error!' She glared at me as if she had just bitten off a piece of lemon. OK, I sometimes go overboard on the subject, itself an error called *déformation professionnelle* (see chapter 92). 'We have spent the $30 regardless of whether we stay or leave, so this factor should not play a role in our decision,' I said, desperately trying to clarify the situation. Needless to say, I gave in in the end and sank back down in my seat.

The next day, I sat in a marketing meeting. Our advertising campaign had been running for four months and had not met even one of its goals. I was in favour of scrapping it. The advertising manager resisted, saying: 'But we've invested so much money in it. If we stop now, it'll all have been for nothing.' Another victim of the *sunk cost fallacy*.

A friend struggled for years in a troubled relationship. His girlfriend cheated on him time and again. Each time, she came back repentant and begged for forgiveness. He explained it to me this way: 'I've invested so much energy in the relationship, it would be wrong to throw it away.' A classic case of the *sunk cost fallacy*.

The *sunk cost fallacy* is most dangerous when we have invested a lot of time, money, energy or love in something. This investment becomes a reason to carry on, even if we are dealing with a lost cause. The more we invest, the greater the sunk costs are, and the greater the urge to continue becomes.

Investors frequently fall victim to the *sunk cost fallacy*. Often they base their trading decisions on acquisition prices. 'I lost so much money with this stock, I can't sell it now,' they say. This is irrational. The acquisition price should play no role. What counts is the stock's future performance (and the future performance of alternative investments). Ironically, the more money a share loses, the more investors tend to stick by it.

This irrational behaviour is driven by a need for consistency. After all, consistency signifies credibility. We find contradictions abominable. If we decide to cancel a project halfway through, we create a contradiction: we admit that we once thought differently. Carrying on with a meaningless project delays this painful realisation and keeps up appearances.

Concorde is a prime example of a government deficit project. Even though both parties, Britain and France, had long known that the supersonic aircraft business would never work, they continued to invest enormous sums of money in it – if only to save face. Abandoning the project would have been tantamount to admitting defeat. The *sunk cost fallacy* is therefore often referred to as the *Concorde effect*. It leads to costly, even disastrous errors of judgement. The Americans extended their involvement in the

Vietnam War because of this. Their thinking: 'We've already sacrificed so much for this war; it'd be a mistake to give up now.'

'We've come this far . . .' 'I've read so much of this book already . . .' 'But I've spent two years doing this course . . .' If you recognise any of these thought patterns, it shows that the *sunk cost fallacy* is at work in a corner of your brain.

Of course, there may be good reasons to continue investing in something to finalise it. But beware of doing so for the wrong reasons, such as to justify non-recoverable investments. Rational decision-making requires you to forget about the costs incurred to date. No matter how much you have already invested, only your assessment of the future costs and benefits counts.

See also **The It'll-Get-Worse-Before-It-Gets-Better Fallacy** (ch.12); **Inability to Close Doors** (ch. 68); **Endowment Effect** (ch. 23); **Effort Justification** (ch. 60); **Loss Aversion** (ch. 32); **Outcome Bias** (ch. 20)

6

DON'T ACCEPT FREE DRINKS

Reciprocity

Not so long ago, you may have come across disciples of the Hare Krishna sect floating around in saffron-coloured robes as you hurried to catch a flight or a train to your destination. A member of the sect presented you with a small flower and a smile. If you're like most people, you took the flower, if only not to be rude. If you tried to refuse, you would have heard a gentle 'Take it, this is our gift to you.' If you wanted to dispose of the flower in the next trashcan, you found that there were already a few there. But that was not the end. Just as your bad conscience started to tug at you, another disciple of Krishna approached you, this time asking for a donation. In many cases, this plea was successful – and so pervasive that many airports banned the sect from the premises.

Psychologist Robert Cialdini can explain the success of this and other such campaigns. He has studied the phenomenon of *reciprocity* and has established that people have extreme difficulty being in another person's debt.

Many NGOs and philanthropic organisations use exactly the same techniques: first give, then take. Last week, a conservation organisation sent me an envelope full of postcards featuring all sorts of idyllic landscapes. The accompanying letter assured me that the postcards were a gift to be kept, whether or not I decided to donate to their organisation. Even though I understood the tactic, it took a little willpower and ruthlessness to throw them in the trash.

Unfortunately, this kind of gentle blackmail – you could also call it corruption – is widespread. A supplier of screws invites a potential customer to join him at a big sports game. A month later, it's time to order screws. The desire not to be in debt is so strong that the buyer gives in and places an order with his new friend.

It is also an ancient technique. We find *reciprocity* in all species whose food supplies are subject to high fluctuations. Suppose you are a hunter-gatherer. One day you are lucky and kill a deer. You can't possibly eat all of it in a day, and refrigerators are still a few centuries away. You decide to share the deer with the group, which ensures that you will benefit from others' spoils when your haul is less impressive. The bellies of your buddies serve as your refrigerator.

Reciprocity is a very useful survival strategy, a form of risk management. Without it, humanity – and countless species of animal – would be long extinct. It is at the core of cooperation between people who are not related to each other and a necessary ingredient for economic growth and wealth creation. There would be no global economy without it – there would be no economy at all. That's the good side of *reciprocity*.

But there is also an ugly side of *reciprocity*: retaliation. Revenge breeds counter-revenge and you soon find yourself in a full-scale war. Jesus preached that we should break this cycle by turning the other cheek, which proves very difficult to do. So compelling is the pull of *reciprocity* even when the stakes are far less high.

Several years ago, a couple invited me and my wife to dinner. We had known this couple casually for quite some time. They were nice, but far from entertaining. We couldn't think of a good excuse to refuse, so we accepted. Things played out exactly as we had imagined: the dinner party was beyond tedious. Nevertheless, we felt obliged to invite them to our home a few months later. The constraint of *reciprocity* had now presented us with two wearisome evenings. And, lo and behold, a few weeks later a follow-up invitation from them arrived. I wonder how many dinner parties have been endured in the name of *reciprocity*, even if the participants would have preferred to drop out of the vicious cycle years ago.

In much the same way, if someone approaches you in the supermarket, whether to offer you a taste of wine, a chunk of cheese or a handful of olives, my best advice is to refuse their offer – unless you want to end up with a refrigerator full of stuff you don't even like.

See also **Framing** (ch. 42); **Incentive Super-Response Tendency** (ch. 18); **Liking Bias** (ch. 22); **Motivation Crowding** (ch. 56)

7

BEWARE THE 'SPECIAL CASE'

Confirmation Bias (Part 1)

Gil wants to lose weight. He selects a particular diet and checks his progress on the scales every morning. If he has lost weight, he pats himself on the back and considers the diet a success. If he has gained weight, he writes it off as a normal fluctuation and forgets about it. For months, he lives under the illusion that the diet is working, even though his weight remains constant. Gil is a victim of the *confirmation bias* – albeit a harmless form of it.

The *confirmation bias* is the mother of all misconceptions. It is the tendency to interpret new information so that it becomes compatible with our existing theories, beliefs and convictions. In other words, we filter out any new information that contradicts our existing views ('disconfirming evidence'). This is a dangerous practice. 'Facts do not cease to exist because they are ignored,' said writer Aldous Huxley. However, we do exactly that, as super-investor Warren Buffett knows: 'What the human being is best at doing, is interpreting all new information so that their prior conclusions remain intact.'

The *confirmation bias* is alive and well in the business world. One example: an executive team decides on a new strategy. The team enthusiastically celebrates any sign that the strategy is a success. Everywhere the executives look, they see plenty of confirming evidence, while indications to the contrary remain unseen or are quickly dismissed as 'exceptions' or 'special cases'. They have become blind to disconfirming evidence.

What can you do? If the word 'exception' crops up, prick up your ears. Often it hides the presence of disconfirming evidence. It pays to listen to Charles Darwin: from his youth, he set out systematically to fight the *confirmation bias*. Whenever observations contradicted his theory, he took them very seriously and noted them down immediately. He knew that the brain actively 'forgets' disconfirming evidence after a short time. The more correct he judged his theory to be, the more actively he looked for contradictions.

The following experiment shows how much effort it takes to question your own theory. A professor presented his students with the number sequence 2–4–6. They had to calculate the underlying rule that the professor had written on the back of a sheet of paper. The students had to provide the next number in the sequence, to which the professor would reply 'fits the rule' or 'does not fit the rule'. The students could guess as many numbers as they wanted, but could try to identify the rule only once. Most students suggested 8 as the next number, and the professor replied: 'Fits the rule.' To be sure, they tried 10, 12 and 14. The professor replied each time: 'Fits the rule.' The students concluded that: 'The rule is to add two to the last number.' The professor shook his head: 'That is not the rule.'

One shrewd student tried a different approach. He tested out the number -2. The professor said 'Does not fit the rule.' 'Seven?' he asked. 'Fits the rule.' The student tried all sorts of numbers -24, 9, -43 . . . Apparently he had an idea, and he was trying to find a flaw with it. Only when he could no longer find a counter-example, the student said: 'The rule is this: the next number must be higher than the previous one.' The professor turned over the sheet of paper, and this was exactly what he'd written down.

What distinguished the resourceful student from the others? While the majority of students sought merely to confirm their theories, he tried to find fault with his, consciously looking for disconfirming evidence. You might think: 'Good for him, but not the end of the world for the others.' However, falling for the *confirmation bias* is not a petty intellectual offence. How it affects our lives will be revealed in the next chapter.

See also **Availability Bias** (ch. 11); **Feature-Positive Effect** (ch. 95); **Coincidence** (ch. 24); **Forer Effect** (ch. 64); **Illusion of Attention** (ch. 88)

8

MURDER YOUR DARLINGS

Confirmation Bias (Part 2)

In the previous chapter, we met the father of all fallacies, the *confirmation bias*. We are forced to establish beliefs about the world, our lives, the economy, investments, our careers and more. We deal mostly in assumptions, and the more nebulous these are, the stronger the *confirmation bias*. Whether you go through life believing that 'people are inherently good' or 'people are inherently bad', you will find daily proof to support your case. Both parties, the philanthropists and the misanthropes, simply filter disconfirming evidence (evidence to the contrary) and focus instead on the do-gooders and dictators who support their worldviews.

Astrologers and economists operate on the same principle. They utter prophecies so vague that any event can substantiate them: 'In the coming weeks you will experience sadness,' or 'in the medium term, the pressure on the dollar will increase.' But what is the medium term? What will cause the dollar to depreciate? And, depreciation measured against what – gold, yen, pesos, wheat, residential property in Manhattan, the average price of a hot dog?

Religious and philosophical beliefs represent an excellent breeding ground for the *confirmation bias*. Here, in soft, spongy terrain, it grows wild and free. For example, worshippers always find evidence for God's existence, even though he never shows himself overtly – except to illiterates in the desert and in isolated mountain villages. It is never to the masses in, say, Frankfurt or New York. Counter-arguments are dismissed by the faithful, demonstrating just how powerful the *confirmation bias* is.

No professionals suffer more from the *confirmation bias* than business journalists. Often, they formulate an easy theory, pad it out with two or three pieces of 'evidence' and call it a day. For example: 'Google is so successful because the company nurtures a culture of creativity.' Once this idea is on paper, the journalist corroborates it by mentioning a few other prosperous companies that foster ingenuity. Rarely does the writer seek out disconfirming evidence, which in this instance would be struggling businesses that live and breathe creativity or, conversely, flourishing firms that are utterly uncreative. Both groups have plenty of members, but the journalist simply ignores them. If he or she were to mention just one, the storyline would be ruined.

Self-help and get-rich-quick books are further examples of blinkered storytelling. Their shrewd authors collect piles of proof to pump up the most banal of theories, such as 'meditation is the key to happiness.' Any reader seeking disconfirming evidence does so in vain: nowhere in these books do we see people who lead fulfilled lives without meditation, or those who, despite meditation, are still sad.

The Internet is particularly fertile ground for the *confirmation bias*. To stay informed, we browse news sites and blogs, forgetting that our favoured pages mirror our existing values, be they liberal, conservative or somewhere in between. Moreover, a lot of sites now tailor content to personal interests and browsing history, causing new and divergent opinions to vanish from the radar altogether. We inevitably land in communities of like-minded people, further reinforcing our convictions – and the *confirmation bias*.

Literary critic Arthur Quiller-Couch had a memorable motto: 'Murder your darlings.' This was his advice to writers who struggled with cutting cherished but redundant sentences. Quiller-Couch's appeal is not just for hesitant hacks, but for all of us who suffer from the deafening silence of assent. To fight against the *confirmation bias*, try writing down your beliefs – whether in terms of worldview, investments, marriage, healthcare, diet, career strategies – and set out to find disconfirming evidence. Axeing beliefs that feel like old friends is hard work, but imperative.

See also **Introspection Illusion** (ch. 67); **Salience Effect** (ch. 83); **Cognitive Dissonance** (ch. 50); **Forer Effect** (ch. 64); **News Illusion** (ch. 99)

9

DON'T BOW TO AUTHORITY

Authority Bias

The first book of the Bible explains what happens when we disobey a great authority: we get ejected from paradise. This is also what less celestial authorities would have us believe – political pundits, scientists, doctors, CEOs, economists, government heads, sports commentators, consultants and stock market gurus.

Authorities pose two main problems to clear thinking: first, their track records are often sobering. There are about one million trained economists on the planet, and not one of them could accurately predict the timing of the 2008 financial crisis (with the exception of Nouriel Roubini and Nassim Taleb), let alone how the collapse would play out, from the real-estate bubble bursting to credit default swaps collapsing, right through to the full-blown economic crunch. Never has a group of experts failed so spectacularly. The story from the medical world is much the same: up until 1900 it was discernibly wiser for patients to avoid doctor's visits; too often the 'treatment' only worsened the illness, due to poor hygiene and folk practices such as bloodletting.

Psychologist Stanley Milgram demonstrated the *authority bias* most clearly in an experiment in 1961. His subjects were instructed to administer ever-increasing electrical shocks to a person sitting on the other side of a pane of glass. They were told to start with 15 volts, then 30V, 45V and so on, until they reached the maximum – a lethal dose of 450V. In reality, no electrical current was actually flowing; Milgram used an actor to play the role of victim, but those charged with administering the shocks didn't know that. The results were, well, shocking: as the person in the other room wailed and writhed in pain, and the subject administering the shock wanted to stop, the professor would say, 'Keep going, the experiment depends on it.' The majority of people continued with the electrocution. More than half of the participants went all the way up to maximum voltage – out of sheer obedience to authority.

Over the past decade, airlines have also learned the dangers of the *authority bias*. In the old days, the captain was king. His commands were not to be doubted. If a co-pilot suspected an oversight, he wouldn't have dared to address it out of respect for – or fear of – his captain. Since this behaviour was discovered, nearly every airline has instituted 'Crew Resource Management' (CRM), which coaches pilots and their crews to discuss any reservations they have openly and quickly. In other words: they carefully deprogramme the *authority bias*. CRM has contributed more to flight safety in the past twenty years than any technical advances have.

Many companies are light years from this sort of foresight. Especially at risk are firms with domineering CEOs, where employees are likely to keep their 'lesser' opinions to themselves – much to the detriment of the business.

Authorities crave recognition and constantly find ways to reinforce their status. Doctors and researchers sport white coats. Bank directors don suits and ties. Kings wear crowns. Members of the military wield rank badges. Today, even more symbols and props are used to signal expertise: from appearances on talk shows and on the covers of magazines, to book tours and their own Wikipedia entries. Authority changes much like fashion does, and society follows it just as much.

In conclusion: whenever you are about to make a decision, think about which authority figures might be exerting an influence on your reasoning. And when you encounter one in the flesh, do your best to challenge him or her.

See also **Twaddle Tendency** (ch. 57); **Chauffeur Knowledge** (ch. 16); **Forecast Illusion** (ch. 40); **Illusion of Skill** (ch. 94)

10

LEAVE YOUR SUPERMODEL FRIENDS AT HOME

Contrast Effect

In his book *Influence*, Robert Cialdini tells the story of two brothers, Sid and Harry, who ran a clothing store in 1930s America. Sid was in charge of sales and Harry led the tailoring department. Whenever Sid noticed that the customers who stood before the mirror really liked their suits, he became a little hard of hearing. He would call to his brother: 'Harry, how much for this suit?' Harry would look up from his cutting table and shout back: 'For that beautiful cotton suit, $42.' (This was a completely inflated price at that time.) Sid would pretend he hadn't understood: 'How much?' Harry would yell again: 'Forty-two dollars!' Sid would then turn to his customer and report: 'He says $22.' At this point, the customer would have quickly put the money on the table and hastened from the store with the suit before poor Sid noticed his 'mistake'.

Maybe you know the following experiment from your schooldays: take two buckets. Fill the first with lukewarm water and the second with ice water. Dip your right hand into the ice water for one minute. Then put both hands into the lukewarm water. What do you notice? The lukewarm water feels as it should to the left hand but piping hot to the right hand.

Both of these stories epitomise the *contrast effect*: we judge something to be beautiful, expensive or large if we have something ugly, cheap or small in front of us. We have difficulty with absolute judgements.

The *contrast effect* is a common misconception. You order leather seats for your new car because compared to the $60,000 price tag on the car, $3,000 seems a pittance. All industries that offer upgrade options exploit this illusion.

The *contrast effect* is at work in other places, too. Experiments show that people are willing to walk an extra ten minutes to save $10 on food. But those same people wouldn't dream of walking ten minutes to save $10 on a thousand-dollar suit. An irrational move because ten minutes is ten minutes, and $10 is $10. Logically, you should walk back in both cases or not at all.

Without the *contrast effect*, the discount business would be completely untenable. A product that has been reduced from $100 to $70 seems better value than a product that has always cost $70. The starting price should play no role. The other day an investor told me: 'The share is a great value because it's 50 per cent below the peak price.' I shook my head. A share price is never 'low' or 'high'. It is what it is, and the only thing that matters is whether it goes up or down from that point.

When we encounter contrasts, we react like birds to a gunshot: we jump up and get moving. Our weak spot: we don't notice small, gradual changes. A magician can make your watch vanish because, when he presses on one part of your body, you don't notice the lighter touch on your wrist as he relieves you of your Rolex. Similarly, we fail to notice how our money disappears. It constantly loses its value, but we do not notice because inflation happens over time. If it were imposed on us in the form of a brutal tax (and basically that's what it is), we would be outraged.

The *contrast effect* can ruin your whole life: a charming woman marries a fairly average man. But because her parents were awful people, the ordinary man appears to be a prince.

One final thought: bombarded by advertisements featuring supermodels, we now perceive beautiful people as only moderately attractive. If you are seeking a partner, never go out in the company of your supermodel friends. People will find you less attractive than you really are. Go alone or, better yet, take two ugly friends.

> *See also* **Availability Bias** (ch. 11); **Endowment Effect** (ch. 23); **Halo Effect** (ch. 38); **Social Comparison Bias** (ch. 72); **Regression to Mean** (ch. 19); **Scarcity Error** (ch. 27); **Framing** (ch. 42)

11

WHY WE PREFER A WRONG MAP TO NO MAP AT ALL

Availability Bias

'Smoking can't be that bad for you: my grandfather smoked three packs of cigarettes a day and lived to be more than 100.' Or: 'Manhattan is really safe. I know someone who lives in the middle of the Village and he never locks his door. Not even when he goes on vacation, and his apartment has never been broken into.' We use statements like these to try to prove something, but they actually prove nothing at all. When we speak like this, we succumb to the *availability bias*.

Are there more English words that start with a K or more words with K as their third letter? Answer: more than twice as many English words have K in third position than start with a K. Why do most people believe the opposite is true? Because we can think of words beginning with a K more quickly. They are more available to our memory.

The *availability bias* says this: we create a picture of the world using the examples that most easily come to mind. This is absurd, of course, because in reality things don't happen more frequently just because we can conceive of them more easily.

Thanks to the *availability bias*, we travel through life with an incorrect risk map in our heads. Thus, we systematically overestimate the risk of being the victim of a plane crash, a car accident or a murder. And we underestimate the risk of dying from less spectacular means, such as diabetes or stomach cancer. The chances of bomb attacks are much rarer than we think, and the chances of suffering depression are much higher. We attach too much likelihood to spectacular, flashy or loud outcomes. Anything silent or invisible we downgrade in our minds. Our brains imagine show-stopping outcomes more readily than mundane ones. We think dramatically, not quantitatively.

Doctors often fall victim to the *availability bias*. They have their favourite treatments, which they use for all possible cases. More appropriate treatments may exist, but these are in the recesses of the doctors' minds. Consequently they practise what they know. Consultants are no better. If they come across an entirely new case, they do not throw up their hands and sigh: 'I really don't know what to tell you.' Instead they turn to one of their more familiar methods, whether or not it is ideal.

If something is repeated often enough, it gets stored at the forefront of our minds. It doesn't even have to be true. How often did the Nazi leaders have to repeat the term 'the Jewish question' before the masses began to believe that it was a serious problem? You simply have to utter the words 'UFO', 'life energy' or 'karma' enough times before people start to credit them.

The *availability bias* has an established seat at the corporate board's table, too. Board members discuss what management has submitted – usually quarterly figures – instead of more important things, such as a clever move by the competition, a slump in employee motivation or an unexpected change in customer behaviour. They tend not to discuss what's not on the agenda. In addition, people prefer information that is easy to obtain, be it economic data or recipes. They make decisions based on this information rather than on more relevant but harder to obtain information – often with disastrous results. For example, we have known for ten years that the so-called Black–Scholes formula for the pricing of derivative financial products does not work. But we don't have another solution, so we carry on with an incorrect tool. It is as if you were in a foreign city without a map, and then pulled out one for your home town and simply used that. We prefer *wrong* information to *no* information. Thus, the *availability bias* has presented the banks with billions in losses.

What was it that Frank Sinatra sang? 'Oh, my heart is beating wildly/And it's all because you're here/When I'm not near the girl I love/I love the girl I'm near.' A perfect example of the *availability bias*. Fend it off by spending time with people who think differently than you think – people whose experiences and expertise are different than yours. We require others' input to overcome the *availability bias*.

See also **Ambiguity Aversion** (ch. 80); **Illusion of Attention** (ch. 88); **Association Bias** (ch. 48); **Feature-Positive Effect** (ch. 95); **Confirmation Bias** (ch. 7–8); **Contrast Effect** (ch. 10); **Neglect of Probability** (ch. 26)

12

WHY 'NO PAIN, NO GAIN' SHOULD SET ALARM BELLS RINGING

The It'll-Get-Worse-Before-It-Gets-Better Fallacy

A few years ago, I was on vacation in Corsica and fell sick. The symptoms were new to me, and the pain was growing by the day. Eventually I decided to seek help at a local clinic. A young doctor began to inspect me, prodding my stomach, gripping my shoulders and knees and then poking each vertebra. I began to suspect that he had no idea what my problem was, but I wasn't really sure so I simply endured the strange examination. To signal its end, he pulled out his notebook and said: 'Antibiotics. Take one tablet three times a day. It'll get worse before it gets better.' Glad that I now had a treatment, I dragged myself back to my hotel room with the prescription in hand.

The pain grew worse and worse – just as the doctor had predicted. The doctor must have known what was wrong with me after all. But, when the pain hadn't subsided after three days, I called him. 'Increase the dose to five times a day. It's going to hurt for a while more,' he said. After two more days of agony, I finally called the international air ambulance. The Swiss doctor diagnosed appendicitis and operated on me immediately. 'Why did you wait so long?' he asked me after the surgery.

I replied: 'It all happened exactly as the doctor said, so I trusted him.'

'Ah, you fell victim to the it'll-get-worse-before-it-gets-better fallacy. That Corsican doctor had no idea. Probably just the same type of stand-in you find in all the tourist places in high season.'

Let's take another example: a CEO is at his wits' end. Sales are in the toilet, the salespeople are unmotivated, and the marketing campaign has sunk without a trace. In his desperation, he hires a consultant. For $5,000 a day, this man analyses the company and comes back with his findings: 'Your sales department has no vision, and your brand isn't positioned clearly. It's a tricky situation. I can fix it for you – but not overnight. The measures will require sensitivity, and most likely, sales will fall further before things improve.' The CEO hires the consultant. A year later, sales fall, and the same thing happens the next year. Again and again, the consultant stresses that the company's progress corresponds closely to his prediction. As sales continue their slump in the third year, the CEO fires the consultant.

A mere smokescreen, the *It'll-Get-Worse-Before-It-Gets-Better Fallacy* is a variant of the so-called *confirmation bias*. If the problem continues to worsen, the prediction is confirmed. If the situation improves unexpectedly, the customer is happy and the expert can attribute it to his prowess. Either way he wins.

Suppose you are president of a country, and have no idea how to run it. What do you do? You predict 'difficult years' ahead, ask your citizens to 'tighten their belts', and then promise to improve the situation only after this 'delicate stage' of the 'cleansing', 'purification' and 'restructuring'. Naturally you leave the duration and severity of the period open.

The best evidence of this strategy's success is Christianity: its literal followers believe that before we can experience heaven on earth, the world must be destroyed. Disasters, floods, fires, death – they are all part of the larger plan and must take place. Believers will view any deterioration of the situation as confirmation of the prophecy, and any improvement as a gift from God.

In conclusion: if someone says 'It'll get worse before it gets better,' you should hear alarm bells ringing. But beware: situations do exist where things first dip and then improve. For example, a career change requires time and often incorporates loss of pay. The reorganisation of a business also takes time. But in all these cases, we can see relatively quickly if the measures are working. The milestones are clear and verifiable. Look to these rather than to the heavens.

See also **Action Bias** (ch. 43); **Sunk Cost Fallacy** (ch. 5); **Regression to the Mean** (ch. 19)

13

EVEN TRUE STORIES
ARE FAIRYTALES

Story Bias

Life is a muddle, as intricate as a Gordian knot. Imagine that an invisible Martian decides to follow you around with an equally invisible notebook, recording what you do, think and dream. The rundown of your life would consist of entries such as 'drank coffee, two sugars', 'stepped on a thumbtack and swore like a sailor', 'dreamed that I kissed the neighbour', 'booked vacation, Maldives, now nearly out of money', 'found hair sticking out of ear, plucked it straight away' and so on. We like to knit this jumble of details into a neat story. We want our lives to form a pattern that can be easily followed. Many call this guiding principle 'meaning'. If our story advances evenly over the years, we refer to it as 'identity'. 'We try on stories as we try on clothes,' said Max Frisch, a famous Swiss novelist.

We do the same with world history, shaping the details into a consistent story. Suddenly we 'understand' certain things; for example, why the Treaty of Versailles led to the Second World War, or why Alan Greenspan's loose monetary policy created the collapse of Lehman Brothers. We comprehend why the Iron Curtain had to fall or why Harry Potter became a best-seller. Here, we speak about 'understanding', but these things cannot be understood in the traditional sense. We simply build the meaning into them afterward. Stories are dubious entities. They simplify and distort reality, and filter things that don't fit. But apparently we cannot do without them. Why remains unclear. What is clear is that people first used stories to explain the world, before they began to think scientifically, making mythology older than philosophy. This has led to the *story bias*.

In the media, the *story bias* rages like wildfire. For example: a car is driving over a bridge when the structure suddenly collapses. What do we read the next day? We hear the tale of the unlucky driver, where he came from and where he was going. We read his biography: born somewhere, grew up somewhere else, earned a living as something. If he survives and can give interviews, we hear exactly how it felt when the bridge came crashing down. The absurd thing: not one of these stories explains the underlying cause of the accident. Skip past the driver's account and consider the bridge's construction: where was the weak point? Was it fatigue? If not, was the bridge damaged? If so, by what? Was a proper design even used? Where are there other bridges of the same design? The problem with all these questions is that, though valid, they just don't make for a good yarn. Stories attract us; abstract details repel us. Consequently, entertaining side issues and backstories are prioritised over relevant facts. (On the upside, if it were not for this, we would be stuck with only non-fiction books.)

Here are two stories from the English novelist E. M. Forster. Which one would you remember better? A) 'The king died, and the queen died.' B) 'The king died, and the queen died of grief.' Most people will retain the second story more easily. Here, the two deaths don't just take place successively; they are emotionally linked. Story A is a factual report, but story B has 'meaning'. According to information theory, we should be able to hold on to A better: it is shorter. But our brains don't work that way.

Advertisers have learned to capitalise on this too. Instead of focusing on an item's benefits, they create a story around it. Objectively speaking, narratives are irrelevant, but still we find them irresistible. Google illustrated this masterfully in its Super Bowl commercial from 2010, 'Google Parisian Love'. Take a look at it on YouTube.

From our own life stories to global events, we shape everything into meaningful stories. Doing so distorts reality and affects the quality of our decisions, but there is a remedy: pick these apart. Ask yourself: what are they trying to hide? Visit the library and spend half a day reading old newspapers. You will see that events that today look connected weren't so at the time. To experience the effect once more, try to view your life story out of context. Dig into your old journals and notes, and you'll see that your life has not followed a straight arrow leading to today, but has been a series of unplanned, unconnected events and experiences, as we'll see in the next chapter.

Whenever you hear a story, ask yourself: who is the sender, what are his intentions and what did he hide under the rug? The omitted elements might not be of relevance. But then again, they might be even more relevant than the elements featured in the story, such as when 'explaining' a financial crisis or the 'cause' of war. The real issue with stories: they give us a false sense of understanding, which inevitably leads us to take bigger risks and urges us to take a stroll on thin ice.

See also **False Causality** (ch.37); **'Because' Justification** (ch. 52); **Personification** (ch. 87); **Hindsight Bias** (ch. 14); **Fundamental Attribution Error** (ch. 36); **Conjunction Fallacy** (ch. 41); **Falsification of History** (ch. 78); **Cherry-Picking** (ch. 96); **News Illusion** (ch. 99)

14

WHY YOU SHOULD KEEP
A DIARY

Hindsight Bias

I came across the diaries of my great-uncle recently. In
1932, he emigrated from a tiny Swiss village to Paris to seek
his fortune in the movie industry. In August 1940, two
months after Paris was occupied, he noted: 'Everyone is
certain that the Germans will leave by the end of the year.
Their officers also confirmed this to me. England will fall
as fast as France did, and then we will finally have our
Parisian lives back – albeit as part of Germany.' The occupation lasted four years.

In today's history books, the German occupation of
France seems to form part of a clear military strategy. In
retrospect, the actual course of the war appears the most
likely of all scenarios. Why? Because we have fallen victim
to the *hindsight bias*.

Let's take a more recent example: in 2007, economic
experts painted a rosy picture for the coming years.
However, just twelve months later, the financial markets
imploded. Asked about the crisis, the same experts enumer-
ated its causes: monetary expansion under Greenspan, lax
validation of mortgages, corrupt rating agencies, low capital requirements, and so forth. In hindsight, the reasons for
the crash seem painfully obvious.

The *hindsight bias* is one of the most prevailing fallacies of all. We can aptly describe it as the 'I told you so' phenomenon: in retrospect, everything seems clear and inevitable. If a CEO becomes successful due to fortunate circumstances he will, looking back, rate the probability of his success a lot higher than it actually was. Similarly, following Ronald Reagan's massive election victory over Jimmy Carter in 1980, commentators announced his appointment to be foreseeable, even though the election lay on a knife-edge until a few days before the final vote. Today, business journalists opine that Google's dominance was predestined, even though each of them would have snorted had such a prediction been made in 1998. One particularly blundering example: nowadays it seems tragic, yet completely plausible, that a single shot in Sarajevo in 1914 would totally upturn the world for thirty years and cost 50 million lives. Every child learns this historical detail in school. But back then, nobody would have dreamed of such an escalation. It would have sounded too absurd.

So why is the *hindsight bias* so perilous? Well, it makes us believe we are better predictors than we actually are, causing us to be arrogant about our knowledge and consequently to take too much risk. And not just with global issues: 'Have you heard? Sylvia and Chris aren't together any more. It was always going to go wrong, they were just so different.' Or: 'They were just so similar.' Or: 'They spent too much time together.' Or even: 'They barely saw one another.'

Overcoming the *hindsight bias* is not easy. Studies have shown that people who are aware of it fall for it just as much as everyone else. So, I'm very sorry, but you've just wasted your time reading this chapter.

If you're still with me, I have one final tip, this time from personal rather than professional experience: keep a journal. Write down your predictions – for political changes, your career, your weight, the stock market and so on. Then, from time to time, compare your notes with actual developments. You will be amazed at what a poor forecaster you are. Don't forget to read history too – not the retrospective, compacted theories compiled in textbooks, but the diaries, oral histories and historical documents from the period. If you can't live without news, read newspapers from five, ten or twenty years ago. This will give you a much better sense of just how unpredictable the world is. Hindsight may provide temporary comfort to those overwhelmed by complexity, but as for providing deeper revelations about how the world works, you'll benefit by looking elsewhere.

See also **Fallacy of the Single Cause** (ch. 97); **Falsification of History** (ch. 78); **Story Bias** (ch. 13); **Forecast Illusion** (ch. 40); **Outcome Bias** (ch. 20); **Self-Serving Bias** (ch. 45)

15

WHY YOU SYSTEMATICALLY OVERESTIMATE YOUR KNOWLEDGE AND ABILITIES

Overconfidence Effect

My favourite musician, Johann Sebastian Bach, was anything but a one-hit wonder. He composed numerous works. How many there were I will reveal at the end of this chapter. But for now, here's a small assignment: how many concertos do you think Bach composed? Choose a range, for example, between 100 and 500, aiming for an estimate that is 98% correct and only 2% off.

How much confidence should we have in our own knowledge? Psychologists Howard Raiffa and Marc Alpert, wondering the same thing, have interviewed hundreds of people in this way. They have asked participants to estimate the total egg production in the U.S., or the number of physicians and surgeons listed in the Yellow Pages of the phone directory for Boston, or the number of foreign automobiles imported into the U.S., or even the toll collections of the Panama Canal in millions of dollars. Subjects could choose any range they liked, with the aim of not being wrong more than 2% of the time. The results were amazing. In the final tally, instead of just 2%, they were off 40% of the time. The researchers dubbed this amazing phenomenon *overconfidence*.

Overconfidence also applies to forecasts, such as stock market performance over a year or your firm's profits over three years. We systematically overestimate our knowledge and our ability to predict – on a massive scale. The *overconfidence effect* does not deal with whether single estimates are correct or not. Rather, as Taleb puts it, it measures the difference between what people actually know and how much they *think* they know. What's surprising is this: experts suffer even more from *overconfidence* than laypeople do. If asked to forecast oil prices in five years' time, an economics professor will be as wide of the mark as a zookeeper will. However, the professor will offer his forecast with certitude.

Overconfidence does not stop at economics: According to Taleb, 84% of Frenchmen estimate that they are above-average lovers. Without the *overconfidence effect*, that figure should be exactly 50% – after all, the statistical 'median' means 50% should rank higher and 50% should rank lower. In another survey, 93% of the U.S. students asked estimated themselves to be 'above average' drivers. And 68% of the faculty at the University of Nebraska rated themselves in the top 25% for teaching ability. Entrepreneurs and those wishing to marry also deem themselves to be different: they believe they can beat the odds. In fact, entrepreneurial activity would be a lot lower if *overconfidence* did not exist. For example, every restaurateur hopes to establish the next Michelin-starred restaurant, even though statistics show that most close their doors after just three years. The return on investment in the restaurant business lies chronically below zero.

Hardly any major projects exist that are completed in less time and at a lower cost than forecasted. Some delays and cost overruns are even legendary, such as the Airbus

A400M, the Sydney Opera House and Boston's Big Dig. The list can be added to at will. Why is that? Here, two effects act in unison. First, you have classic *overconfidence*. Second, those with a direct interest in the project have an incentive to underestimate the costs: consultants, contractors and suppliers seek follow-up orders. Builders feel bolstered by the optimistic figures and, through their activities, politicians get more votes. We will examine this *strategic misrepresentation* (Chapter 89) later in the book.

What makes *overconfidence* so prevalent and its effect so confounding is that it is not driven by incentives; it is raw and innate. And it's not counterbalanced by the opposite effect, 'underconfidence', which doesn't exist. No surprise to some readers: *overconfidence* is more pronounced in men – women tend not to overestimate their knowledge and abilities as much. Even more troubling: optimists are not the only victims of *overconfidence*. Even self-proclaimed pessimists overrate themselves – just less extremely.

In conclusion: be aware that you tend to overestimate your knowledge. Be sceptical of predictions, especially if they come from so-called experts. And with all plans, favour the pessimistic scenario. This way you have a chance of judging the situation somewhat realistically.

Back to the question from the beginning: Johann Sebastian Bach composed 1127 works that survived to this day. He may have composed considerably more, but they are lost.

See also **Illusion of Skill** (ch. 94); **Forecast Illusion** (ch. 40); **Strategic Misrepresentation** (ch. 89); **Incentive Super-Response Tendency** (ch. 18); **Self-Serving Bias** (ch. 45)

16

DON'T TAKE NEWS ANCHORS SERIOUSLY

Chauffeur Knowledge

After receiving the Nobel Prize for Physics in 1918, Max Planck went on tour across Germany. Wherever he was invited, he delivered the same lecture on new quantum mechanics. Over time, his chauffeur grew to know it by heart: 'It has to be boring giving the same speech each time, Professor Planck. How about I do it for you in Munich? You can sit in the front row and wear my chauffeur's cap. That'd give us both a bit of variety.' Planck liked the idea, so that evening the driver held a long lecture on quantum mechanics in front of a distinguished audience. Later, a physics professor stood up with a question. The driver recoiled: 'Never would I have thought that someone from such an advanced city as Munich would ask such a simple question! My chauffeur will answer it.'

According to Charlie Munger, one of the world's best investors (and from whom I have borrowed this story), there are two types of knowledge. First, we have *real* knowledge. We see it in people who have committed a large amount of time and effort to understanding a topic. The second type is *chauffeur knowledge* – knowledge from people who have learned to put on a show. Maybe they have a great voice or good hair, but the knowledge they espouse is not their own. They reel off eloquent words as if reading from a script.

Unfortunately, it is increasingly difficult to separate true knowledge from *chauffeur knowledge*. With news anchors, however, it is still easy. These are actors. Period. Everyone knows it. And yet it continues to astound me how much respect these perfectly-coiffed script readers enjoy, not to mention how much they earn moderating panels about topics they barely fathom.

With journalists, it is more difficult. Some have acquired true knowledge. Often they are veteran reporters who have specialised for years in a clearly defined area. They make a serious effort to understand the complexity of a subject and to communicate it. They tend to write long articles that highlight a variety of cases and exceptions. The major-ity of journalists, however, fall into the category of chauffeur. They conjure up articles off the tops of their heads, or rather, from Google searches. Their texts are one-sided, short, and – often as compensation for their patchy knowledge – snarky and self-satisfied in tone.

The same superficiality is present in business. The larger a company, the more the CEO is expected to possess 'star quality'. Dedication, solemnity, and reliability are under-valued, at least at the top. Too often shareholders and business journalists seem to believe that showmanship will deliver better results, which is obviously not the case.

To guard against the chauffeur effect, Warren Buffett, Munger's business partner, has coined a wonderful phrase, 'circle of competence'. What lies inside this circle you understand intuitively; what lies outside, you may only partially comprehend. One of Munger's best pieces of advice is: 'You have to stick within what I call your circle of competence. You have to know what you understand and what you don't understand. It's not terribly important how big the circle is. But it is terribly important that you know where the perimeter is.' Munger underscores this: 'So you have to figure out what your own aptitudes are. If you play games where other people have the aptitudes and you don't, you're going to lose. And that's as close to certain as any prediction that you can make. You have to figure out where you've got an edge. And you've got to play within your own circle of competence.'

In conclusion: be on the lookout for *chauffeur knowledge*. Do not confuse the company spokesperson, the ringmaster, the newscaster, the schmoozer, the verbiage vendor or the cliché generator with those who possess true knowledge. How do you recognise the difference? There is a clear indicator: true experts recognise the limits of what they know and what they do not know. If they find themselves outside their circle of competence, they keep quiet or simply say, 'I don't know.' This they utter unapologetically, even with a certain pride. From chauffeurs, we hear every line except this.

See also **Authority Bias** (ch. 9); **Domain Dependence** (ch. 76); **Twaddle Tendency** (ch. 57)

17

YOU CONTROL LESS THAN YOU THINK

Illusion of Control

Every day, shortly before nine o'clock, a man with a red hat stands in a square and begins to wave his cap around wildly. After five minutes he disappears. One day, a policeman comes up to him and asks: 'What are you doing?' 'I'm keeping the giraffes away.' 'But there aren't any giraffes here.' 'Well, I must be doing a good job, then.'

A friend with a broken leg was stuck in bed and asked me to pick up a lottery ticket for him. I went to the store, checked a few boxes, wrote his name on it and paid. As I handed him the copy of the ticket, he balked. 'Why did *you* fill it out? I wanted to do that. I'm never going to win anything with your numbers!'

'Do you really think it affects the draw if *you* pick the numbers?' I inquired. He looked at me blankly.

In casinos, most people throw the dice as hard as they can if they need a high number, and as gingerly as possible if they are hoping for a low number – which is as nonsensical as football fans thinking they can swing a game by gesticulating in front of the TV. Unfortunately they share this illusion with many people who also seek to influence the world by sending out the 'right' thoughts (vibrations, positive energy, karma . . .).

The *illusion of control* is the tendency to believe that we can influence something over which we have absolutely no sway. This was discovered in 1965 by two researchers, Jenkins and Ward. Their experiment was simple, consisting of just two switches and a light. The men were able to adjust when the switches connected to the light and when not. Even when the light flashed on and off at random, subjects were still convinced that they could influence it by flicking the switches.

Or consider this example: an American researcher has been investigating acoustic sensitivity to pain. For this, he placed people in sound booths and increased the volume until the subjects signalled him to stop. The two rooms, A and B, were identical, save one thing: room B had a red panic button on the wall. The button was purely for show, but it gave participants the feeling that they were in control of the situation, leading them to withstand significantly more noise. If you have read Aleksandr Solzhenitsyn, Primo Levi or Viktor Frankl, this finding will not surprise you: the idea that people can influence their destiny even by a fraction encouraged these prisoners not to give up hope.

Crossing the street in Los Angeles is a tricky business, but luckily, at the press of a button, we can stop traffic. Or can we? The button's real purpose is to make us believe we have an influence on the traffic lights, and thus we're better able to endure the wait for the signal to change with more patience. The same goes for 'door-open' and 'door-close' buttons in elevators: many are not even connected to the electrical panel. Such tricks are also designed into open-plan offices: for some people it will always be too hot, for others too cold. Clever technicians create the *illusion of control* by installing fake temperature dials. This reduces energy bills – and complaints. Such ploys are called 'placebo buttons' and they are being pushed in all sorts of realms.

Central bankers and government officials employ placebo buttons masterfully. Take, for instance, the federal funds rate, which is an extreme short-term rate, an overnight rate to be precise. While this rate doesn't affect long-term interest rates (which are a function of supply and demand, and an important factor in investment decisions), the stock market, nevertheless, reacts frenetically to its every change. Nobody understands why overnight interest rates can have such an effect on the market, but everybody thinks they do, and so they do. The same goes for pronouncements made by the Chairman of the Federal Reserve; markets move, even though these statements inject little of tangible value into the real economy. They are merely sound waves. And still we allow economic heads to continue to play with the illusory dials. It would be a real wake-up call if all involved realised the truth – that the world economy is a fundamentally uncontrollable system.

And you? Do you have everything under control? Probably less than you think. Do not think you command your way through life like a Roman emperor. Rather, you are the man with the red hat. Therefore, focus on the few things of importance that you can really influence. For everything else: *que sera, sera.*

See also **Coincidence** (ch. 24); **Neglect of Probability** (ch. 26); **Forecast Illusion** (ch. 40); **Illusion of Skill** (ch. 94); **Clustering Illusion** (ch. 3); **Introspection Illusion** (ch. 67)

18

NEVER PAY YOUR LAWYER BY THE HOUR

Incentive Super-Response Tendency

To control a rat infestation, French colonial rulers in Hanoi in the nineteenth century passed a law: for every dead rat handed in to the authorities, the catcher would receive a reward. Yes, many rats were destroyed, but many were also bred specially for this purpose.

In 1947, when the Dead Sea scrolls were discovered, archaeologists set a finder's fee for each new parchment. Instead of lots of extra scrolls being found, they were simply torn apart to increase the reward. Similarly, in China in the nineteenth century, an incentive was offered for finding dinosaur bones. Farmers located a few on their land, broke them into pieces and cashed in. Modern incentives are no better: company boards promise bonuses for achieved targets. And what happens? Managers invest more energy in trying to lower the targets than in growing the business.

These are examples of the *incentive super-response tendency*. Credited to Charlie Munger, this titanic name describes a rather trivial observation: people respond to incentives by doing what is in their best interests. What is noteworthy is, first, how quickly and radically people's behaviour changes when incentives come into play or are altered and, second, the fact that people respond to the incentives themselves and not the grander intentions behind them.

Good incentive systems comprise both intent and reward. An example: in Ancient Rome, engineers were made to stand *underneath* the construction at their bridges' opening ceremonies. Poor incentive systems, on the other hand, overlook and sometimes even pervert the underlying aim. For example, censoring a book makes its contents more famous and rewarding bank employees for each loan sold leads to a miserable credit portfolio. Making CEOs' pay public didn't dampen the astronomical salaries; to the contrary, it pushed them upward. Nobody wants to be the loser CEO in his industry.

Do you want to influence the behaviour of people or organisations? You could always preach about values and visions, or you could appeal to reason. But in nearly every case, incentives work better. These need not be monetary; anything is useable, from good grades to Nobel Prizes to special treatment in the afterlife.

For a long time I tried to understand what made well-educated nobles from the Middle Ages bid adieu to their comfortable lives, swing themselves up on to horses and take part in the Crusades. They were well aware that the arduous ride to Jerusalem lasted at least six months and passed directly through enemy territory, yet they took the risk. And then it came to me: the answer lies in incentive systems. If they came back alive, they could keep the spoils of war and live out their days as rich men. If they died, they automatically passed on to the afterlife as martyrs – with all the benefits that came with it. It was win-win.

Imagine for a moment that, instead of demanding enemies' riches, warriors and soldiers charged by the hour. We would effectively be incentivising them to take as long as possible, right? So why do we do just this with lawyers, architects, consultants, accountants and driving instructors? My advice: forget hourly rates and always negotiate a fixed price in advance.

Be wary, too, of investment advisers endorsing particular financial products. They are not interested in your financial well-being, but in earning a commission on these products. The same goes for entrepreneurs' and investment bankers' business plans. These are often worthless because, again, the vendors have their own interests at heart. What is the old adage? 'Never ask a barber if you need a haircut.'

In conclusion: keep an eye out for the *incentive super-response tendency*. If a person's or an organisation's behaviour confounds you, ask yourself what incentive might lie behind it. I guarantee you that you'll be able to explain 90% of the cases this way. What makes up the remaining 10%? Passion, idiocy, psychosis or malice.

See also **Motivation Crowding** (ch. 56); **Reciprocity** (ch. 6); **Overconfidence Effect** (ch. 15); **Motivation Crowding** (ch. 56)

19

THE DUBIOUS EFFICACY OF DOCTORS, CONSULTANTS AND PSYCHOTHERAPISTS

Regression to Mean

His back pain was sometimes better, sometimes worse. There were days when he felt like he could move mountains, and those when he could barely move. When that was the case – fortunately it happened only rarely – his wife would drive him to the chiropractor. The next day he would feel much more mobile and would recommend the therapist to everyone.

Another man, younger and with a respectable golf handicap of 12, gushed in a similar fashion about his golf instructor. Whenever he played miserably, he booked an hour with the pro, and lo and behold, in the next game he fared much better.

A third man, an investment adviser at a major bank, invented a sort of 'rain dance', which he performed in the restroom every time his stocks had performed extremely badly. As absurd as it seemed, he felt compelled to do it: and things always improved afterward.

What links the three men is a fallacy: the *regression-to-mean* delusion.

Suppose your region is experiencing a record period of cold weather. In all probability, the temperature will rise in the next few days, back toward the monthly average. The same goes for extreme heat, drought or rain. Weather fluctuates around a mean. The same is true for chronic pain, golf handicaps, stock market performance, luck in love, subjective happiness and test scores. In short, the crippling back pain would most likely have improved without a chiropractor. The handicap would have returned to 12 without additional lessons. And the performance of the investment adviser would also have shifted back toward the market average – with or without the restroom dance.

Extreme performances are interspersed with less extreme ones. The most successful stock picks from the past three years are hardly going to be the most successful stocks in the coming three years. Knowing this, you can appreciate why some athletes would rather not make it on to the front pages of the newspapers: subconsciously they know that the next time they race, they probably won't achieve the same top result – which has nothing to do with the media attention, but is to do with natural variations in performance.

Or, take the example of a division manager who wants to improve employee morale by sending the least motivated 3% of the workforce on a course. The result? The next time he looks at motivation levels, the same people will not make up the bottom few – there will be others. Was the course worth it? Hard to say, since the group's motivation levels would probably have returned to their personal norms even without the training. The situation is similar with patients who are hospitalised for depression. They usually leave the clinic feeling a little better. It is quite possible, however, that the stay contributed absolutely nothing.

Another example: in Boston, the lowest-performing schools were entered into a complex support programme. The following year, the schools had moved up in the rankings, an improvement that the authorities attributed to the programme rather than to natural *regression to mean*.

Ignoring *regression to mean* can have destructive consequences, such as teachers (or managers) concluding that the stick is better than the carrot. For example, following a test the highest performing students are praised, and the lowest are castigated. In the next exam, other students will probably – purely coincidentally – achieve the highest and lowest scores. Thus, the teacher concludes that reproach helps and praise hinders. A fallacy that keeps on giving.

In conclusion: when you hear stories such as: 'I was sick, went to the doctor, and got better a few days later' or 'the company had a bad year, so we got a consultant in and now the results are back to normal', look out for our old friend, the *regression-to-mean* error.

See also **Problem with Averages** (ch. 55); **Contrast Effect** (ch. 10); **The It'll-Get-Worse-Before-It-Gets-Better Fallacy** (ch. 12); **Coincidence** (ch. 24); **Gambler's Fallacy** (ch. 29)

20

NEVER JUDGE A DECISION
BY ITS OUTCOME

Outcome Bias

A quick hypothesis: say one million monkeys speculate on the stock market. They buy and sell stocks like crazy and, of course, completely at random. What happens? After one week, about half of the monkeys will have made a profit and the other half a loss. The ones that made a profit can stay; the ones that made a loss you send home. In the second week, one half of the monkeys will still be riding high, while the other half will have made a loss and are sent home. And so on. After ten weeks, about 1,000 monkeys will be left – those who have always invested their money well. After twenty weeks, just one monkey will remain – this one always, without fail, chose the right stocks and is now a billionaire. Let's call him the success monkey.

How does the media react? They will pounce on this animal to understand its 'success principles'. And they will find some: perhaps the monkey eats more bananas than the others. Perhaps he sits in another corner of the cage. Or, maybe he swings headlong through the branches, or he takes long, reflective pauses while grooming. He must have some recipe for success, right? How else could he perform so brilliantly? Spot-on for twenty weeks – and that from a simple monkey? Impossible!

The monkey story illustrates the *outcome bias*: we tend to evaluate decisions based on the result rather than on the decision process. This fallacy is also known as the *historian error*. A classic example is the Japanese attack on Pearl Harbor. Should the military base have been evacuated or not? From today's perspective: obviously, for there was plenty of evidence that an attack was imminent. However, only in retrospect do the signals appear so clear. At the time, in 1941, there was a plethora of contradictory signals. Some pointed to an attack; others did not. To assess the quality of the decision, we must use the information available at the time, filtering out everything we know about it post-attack (particularly that it did indeed take place).

Another experiment: you must evaluate the performance of three heart surgeons. To do this, you ask each to carry out a difficult operation five times. Over the years, the probability of dying from these procedures has stabilised at 20%. With surgeon A, no one dies. With surgeon B, one patient dies. With surgeon C, two die. How do you rate the performance of A, B and C? If you think like most people, you rate A the best, B the second best, and C the worst. And thus you've just fallen for the *outcome bias*. You can guess why: the samples are too small, rendering the results meaningless. You can only really judge a surgeon if you know something about the field, and then carefully monitor the preparation and execution of the operation. In other words, you assess the process and not the result. Alternatively, you could employ a larger sample, if you have enough patients who need this particular operation: 100 or 1,000 operations. For now it is enough to know that, with an average surgeon, there is a 33% chance that no one will die, a 41% chance that one person will die and a 20%

chance that two people will die. That's a simple probability calculation. What stands out: there is no huge difference between zero dead and two dead. To assess the three surgeons purely on the basis of the outcomes would be not only negligent but also unethical.

In conclusion: never judge a decision purely by its result, especially when randomness or 'external factors' play a role. A bad result does not automatically indicate a bad decision and vice versa. So rather than tearing your hair out about a wrong decision, or applauding yourself for one that may have only coincidentally led to success, remember why you chose what you did. Were your reasons rational and understandable? Then you would do well to stick with that method, even if you didn't strike lucky last time.

See also **Sunk Cost Fallacy** (ch. 5); **Swimmer's Body Illusion** (ch. 2); **Hindsight Bias** (ch. 14); **Illusion of Skill** (ch. 94)

21

LESS IS MORE

The Paradox of Choice

My sister and her husband bought an unfinished house a little while ago. Since then, we haven't been able to talk about anything else. The sole topic of conversation for the past two months has been bathroom tiles: ceramic, granite, marble, metal, stone, wood, glass and every type of laminate known to man. Rarely have I seen my sister in such anguish. 'There are just too many to choose from,' she exclaims, throwing her hands in the air and returning to the tile catalogue, her constant companion.

I've counted and researched: my local grocery store stocks 48 varieties of yogurt, 134 types of red wine, 64 different cleaning products and a grand total of 30,000 items. Amazon, the Internet bookseller, has two million titles available. Nowadays, people are bombarded with options, such as hundreds of mental disorders, thousands of different careers, even more holiday destinations and an infinite variety of lifestyles. There has never been more choice.

When I was young, we had three types of yogurt, three television channels, two churches, two kinds of cheese (mild or strong), one type of fish (trout) and one telephone, provided by the Swiss Post. The black box with the dial served no other purpose than making calls, and that did us just fine. In contrast, anyone who enters a phone store today runs the risk of being flattened by an avalanche of brands, models and contract options.

And yet, selection is the yardstick of progress. It is what sets us apart from planned economies and the Stone Age. Yes, abundance makes you giddy, but there is a limit. When it is exceeded, a surfeit of choices destroys quality of life. The technical term for this is the *paradox of choice*.

In his book of the same title, psychologist Barry Schwartz describes why this is so. First, a large selection leads to inner paralysis. To test this, a supermarket set up a stand where customers could sample twenty-four varieties of jelly. They could try as many as they liked and then buy them at a discount. The next day, the owners carried out the same experiment with only six flavours. The result? They sold ten times more jelly on day two. Why? With such a wide range, customers could not come to a decision, so they bought nothing. The experiment was repeated several times with different products. The results were always the same.

Second, a broader selection leads to poorer decisions. If you ask young people what is important in a life partner, they reel off all the usual qualities: intelligence, good manners, warmth, the ability to listen, a sense of humour and physical attractiveness. But do they actually take these criteria into account when choosing someone? In the past, a young man from a village of average size could choose among maybe twenty girls of similar age with whom he went to school. He knew their families and vice versa, leading to a decision based on several well-known attributes. Nowadays, in the era of online dating, millions of potential partners are at our disposal. It has been proven that the stress caused by this mind-boggling variety is so large that the male brain reduces the decision to one single criterion: physical attractiveness. The consequences of this selection process you already know – perhaps even from personal experience.

Finally, large selection leads to discontent. How can you be sure you are making the right choice when 200 options surround and confound you? The answer is: you cannot. The more choice you have, the more unsure and therefore dissatisfied you are afterward.

So, what can you do? Think carefully about what you want before you inspect existing offers. Write down these criteria and stick to them rigidly. Also, realise that you can never make a perfect decision. Aiming for this, given the flood of possibilities, is a form of irrational perfectionism. Instead, learn to love a 'good' choice. Yes, even in terms of life partners. Only the best will do? In this age of unlimited variety, rather the opposite is true: 'good enough' is the new optimum (except, of course, for you and me).

See also **Decision Fatigue** (ch. 53); **Alternative Blindness** (ch. 71); **Default Effect** (ch. 81)

22

YOU LIKE ME, YOU REALLY REALLY LIKE ME

Liking Bias

Kevin has just bought two boxes of fine Margaux. He rarely drinks wine – not even Bordeaux – but the sales assistant was so nice, not fake or pushy, just really likeable. So he bought them.

Joe Girard is considered the most successful car salesman in the world. His tip for success: 'There's nothing more effective in selling anything than getting the customer to believe, really believe, that you like him and care about him.' Girard doesn't just talk the talk: his secret weapon is sending a card to his customers each month. Just one sentence salutes them: 'I like you.'

The *liking bias* is startlingly simple to understand and yet we continually fall prey to it. It means this: the more we like someone, the more inclined we are to buy from or help that person. Still, the question remains: what does 'likeable' even mean? According to research, we see people as pleasant if A) they are outwardly attractive, B) they are similar to us in terms of origin, personality or interests, and C) they like us. Consequently, advertising is full of attractive people. Ugly people seem unfriendly and don't even make it into the background (see A). In addition to engaging super-attractive types, advertising also employs 'people like you and me' (see B) – those who are similar in appearance, accent or background. In short, the more similar the better. Mirroring is a standard technique in sales to get exactly this effect. Here, the salesperson tries to copy the gestures, language, and facial expressions of his prospective client. If the buyer speaks very slowly and quietly, often scratching his head, it makes sense for the seller to speak slowly and quietly, and to scratch his head now and then too. That makes him likeable in the eyes of the buyer, and thus a business deal is more likely. Finally, it's not unheard of for advertisers to pay us compliments: how many times have you bought something 'because you're worth it'? Here factor C comes into play: we find people appealing if they like us. Compliments work wonders, even if they ring hollow as a drum.

So-called multilevel marketing (selling through personal networks) works solely because of the *liking bias*. Though there are excellent plastic containers in the supermarket for a quarter of the price, Tupperware generates an annual turnover of two billion dollars. Why? The friends who hold the Tupperware parties meet the second and third congeniality standard perfectly.

Aid agencies employ the *liking bias* to great effect. Their campaigns use beaming children or women almost exclusively. Never will you see a stone-faced, wounded guerrilla fighter staring at you from billboards – even though he also needs your support. Conservation organisations also carefully select who gets the starring role in their advertisements. Have you ever seen a World Wildlife Fund brochure filled with spiders, worms, algae or bacteria? They are perhaps just as endangered as pandas, gorillas, koalas and seals – and even more important for the ecosystem. But we feel nothing for them. The more human a creature acts, the more similar it is to us, the more we like it. The bone skipper fly is extinct? Too bad.

Politicians, too, are maestros of the *liking bias*. Depending on the make-up and interests of an audience, they emphasise different topics, such as residential area, social background or economic issues. And they flatter us: Each potential voter is made to feel like an indispensable member of the team: 'Your vote counts!' Of course your vote counts, but only by the tiniest of fractions, bordering on the irrelevant.

A friend who deals in oil pumps told me how he once closed an eight-figure deal for a pipeline in Russia. 'Bribery?' I inquired. He shook his head. 'We were chatting, and suddenly we got on to the topic of sailing. It turned out that both of us – the buyer and me – were die-hard 470 dinghy fans. From that moment on, he liked me; I was a friend. So the deal was sealed. Amiability works better than bribery.'

So, if you are a salesperson, make buyers think you like them, even if this means outright flattery. And if you are a consumer, always judge a product independent of who is selling it. Banish the salespeople from your mind, or rather, pretend you don't like them.

See also **Reciprocity** (ch. 6); **Personification** (ch. 87)

23

DON'T CLING TO THINGS

Endowment Effect

The BMW gleamed in the parking lot of the used-car dealership. Although it had a few miles on the odometer, it looked in perfect condition. I know a little about used cars, and to me it was worth around $40,000. However, the salesman was pushing for $50,000 and wouldn't budge a dime. When he called the next week to say he would accept $40,000 after all, I went for it. The next day, I took it out for a spin and stopped at a gas station. The owner came out to admire the car – and proceeded to offer me $53,000 in cash on the spot. I politely declined. Only on the way home did I realise how ridiculous I was to have said no. Something that I considered worth $40,000 had passed into my possession and suddenly taken on a value of more than $53,000. If I were thinking purely rationally, I would have sold the car immediately. But, alas, I'd fallen under the influence of the *endowment effect*. We consider things to be more valuable the moment we own them. In other words, if we are selling something, we charge more for it than what we ourselves would be willing to spend.

To probe this, psychologist Dan Ariely conducted the following experiment: in one of his classes, he raffled tickets to a major basketball game, then polled the students to see how much they thought the tickets were worth. The empty-handed students estimated around $170, whereas the winning students would not sell their ticket below an average of $2,400. The simple fact of ownership makes us add zeros to the selling price.

In real estate, the *endowment effect* is palpable. Sellers become emotionally attached to their houses and thus systematically overestimate their value. They balk at the market price, expecting buyers to pay more – which is completely absurd since this excess is little more than senti-mental value.

Richard Thaler performed an interesting classroom experiment at Cornell University to measure the *endow-ment effect*. He distributed coffee mugs to half of the students and told them they could either take the mug home or sell it at a price they could specify. The other half of the students, who didn't get a mug, were asked how much they would be willing to pay for a mug. In other words, Thaler set up a market for coffee mugs. One would expect that roughly 50% of the students would be willing to trade – to either sell or buy a mug. But the result was much lower than that. Why? Because the average owner would not sell below $5.25, and the average buyer would not pay more than $2.25 for a mug.

We can safely say that we are better at collecting things than at casting them off. Not only does this explain why we fill our homes with junk, but also why lovers of stamps, watches and pieces of art part with them so seldomly.

Amazingly, the *endowment effect* affects not only possession but also near-ownership. Auction houses like Christie's and Sotheby's thrive on this. A person who bids until the end of an auction gets the feeling that the object is practically theirs, thus increasing its value. The would-be owner is suddenly willing to pay much more than planned, and any withdrawal from the bidding is perceived as a loss – which defies all logic. In large auctions, such as those for mining rights or mobile radio frequencies, we often observe the *winner's curse*: here, the successful bidder turns out to be the economic loser when he gets caught up in the fervour and overbids. I'll offer more insight on the *winner's curse* in chapter 35.

There's a similar effect in the job market. If you are applying for a job and don't get a call back, you have every reason to be disappointed. However, if you make it to the final stages of the selection process and then receive the rejection, the disappointment can be much bigger – irrationally. Either you get the job or you don't; nothing else should matter.

In conclusion: don't cling to things. Consider your property something that the 'universe' (whatever you believe this to be) has bestowed on you temporarily. Keep in mind that it can recoup this (or more) in the blink of an eye.

See also **House-Money Effect** (ch. 84); **Sunk Costs Fallacy** (ch. 5); **Winner's Curse** (ch. 35); **Contrast Effect** (ch. 10); **Loss Aversion** (ch. 32); **Cognitive Dissonance** (ch. 50); **Not-Invented-Here Syndrome** (ch. 74); **Fear of Regret** (ch. 82)

24

THE INEVITABILITY OF UNLIKELY EVENTS

Coincidence

At 7.15p.m. on 1 March 1950, the fifteen members of the church choir in Beatrice, Nebraska were scheduled to meet for rehearsal. For various reasons, they were all running behind. The minister's family was delayed because his wife still had to iron their daughter's dress. One couple was held back when their car wouldn't start. The pianist wanted to be there 30 minutes early, but he fell into a deep sleep after dinner. And so on. At 7.25p.m., the church exploded. The blast was heard all around the village. It blew out the walls and sent the roof crashing to the ground. Miraculously, nobody was killed. The fire chief traced the explosion back to a gas leak, even though members of the choir were convinced they had received a sign from God. Hand of God or *coincidence*?

Something last week made me think of my old school friend, Andy, whom I hadn't spoken to in a long time. Suddenly the phone rang. I picked it up and, lo and behold, it was Andy. 'I must be telepathic!' I exclaimed excitedly. But, telepathy or *coincidence*?

On 5 October 1990, the *San Francisco Examiner* reported that Intel would take its rival, AMD, to court. Intel found out that the company was planning to launch a computer chip named AM386, a term which clearly referred to Intel's 386 chip. How Intel came upon the information is remarkable: by pure coincidence, both companies had hired someone named Mike Webb. Both men were staying in the same hotel in California, and checked out on the same day. After they had left, the hotel accepted a package for Mike Webb at reception. It contained confidential documents about the AM386 chip, and the hotel mistakenly sent it to Mike Webb of Intel, who promptly forwarded the contents to the legal department.

How likely are stories like that? The Swiss psychiatrist C.G. Jung saw in them the work of an unknown force, which he called synchronicity. But how should a rationally minded thinker approach these accounts? Preferably with a piece of paper and a pencil. Consider the first case, the explosion of the church. Draw four boxes to represent each of the potential events. The first possibility is what actually took place: 'choir delayed and church exploded.' But there are three other options: 'choir delayed and church did not explode,' 'choir on time and church exploded' and 'choir on time and church did not explode.' Estimate the frequencies of these events and write them in the corresponding box. Pay special attention to how often the last case has happened: every day, millions of choirs gather for scheduled rehearsals and their churches don't blow up. Suddenly, the story has lost its unimaginable quality. For all these millions of churches, it would be improbable if something like what happened in Beatrice, Nebraska didn't take place at least once a century. So, no: no hand of God. (And anyway, why would God want to blow a church to smithereens? What a ridiculous way to communicate with your worshippers!)

Let's apply the same thinking to the phone call. Keep in mind the many occasions when 'Andy' thinks of you but doesn't call; when you think of him and he doesn't call; when you don't think of him and he calls; when he doesn't think of you and you call . . . There is an almost infinite number of occasions when you don't think of him and he doesn't call. But, since people spend about 90% of their time thinking about others, it is not unlikely that, eventually, two people will think of each other and one of them will pick up the phone. And it must not be just Andy: if you have 100 other friends, the probability of this happening increases greatly.

We tend to stumble when estimating probabilities. If someone says 'never', I usually register this as a minuscule probability greater than zero, since 'never' cannot be compensated by a negative probability.

In sum: let's not get too excited. Improbable coincidences are precisely that: rare but very possible events. It's not surprising when they finally happen. What would be more surprising would be if they never came to be.

See also **False Causality** (ch.37); **Confirmation Bias** (chs. 7–8); **Regression to Mean** (ch. 19); **Illusion of Control** (ch. 17); **Clustering Illusion** (ch. 3)

25

THE CALAMITY OF CONFORMITY

Groupthink

Have you ever bitten your tongue in a meeting? Surely. You sit there, say nothing and nod along to proposals. After all, you don't want to be the (eternal) naysayer. Moreover, you might not be 100% sure why you disagree, whereas the others are unanimous – and far from stupid. So you keep your mouth shut for another day. When everyone thinks and acts like this, *groupthink* is at work: this is where a group of smart people makes reckless decisions because everyone aligns their opinions with the supposed consensus. Thus, motions are passed that each individual group member would have rejected if no peer pressure had been involved. *Groupthink* is a special branch of *social proof*, a flaw that we discussed in chapter 4.

In March 1960, the U.S. Secret Service began to mobilise anti-communist exiles from Cuba, most of them living in Miami, to use against Fidel Castro's regime. In January 1961, two days after taking office, President Kennedy was informed about the secret plan to invade Cuba. Three months later, a key meeting took place at the White House in which Kennedy and his advisers all voted in favour of the invasion. On 17 April 1961, a brigade of 1,400 exiled Cubans landed at the Bay of Pigs, on Cuba's south coast, with the help of the U.S. Navy, the Air Force and the CIA. The aim was to overthrow Castro's government. However, nothing went as planned. On the first day, not a single supply ship reached the coast. The Cuban air force sank the first two and the next two turned around and fled back to the U.S. A day later, Castro's army completely surrounded the brigade. On the third day, the 1,200 survivors were taken into custody and sent to military prisons. Kennedy's invasion of the Bay of Pigs is regarded as one of the biggest flops in American foreign policy. That such an absurd plan was ever agreed upon, never mind put into action, is astounding. All of the assumptions that spoke in favour of invasion were erroneous. For example, Kennedy's team completely underestimated the strength of Cuba's air force. Also, it was expected that, in an emergency, the brigade would be able to hide in the Escambray mountains and carry out an underground war against Castro from there. A glance at the map shows that the refuge was 100 miles away from the Bay of Pigs, with an insurmountable swamp in between. And yet, Kennedy and his advisers were among the most intelligent people to ever run an American government. What went wrong between January and April of 1961?

Psychology professor Irving Janis has studied many fiascos. He concluded that they share the following pattern: members of a close-knit group cultivate team spirit by (unconsciously) building illusions. One of these fantasies is a belief in invincibility: 'If both our leader [in this case, Kennedy] and the group are confident that the plan will work, then luck will be on our side.' Next comes the illusion of unanimity: if the others are of the same opinion, any dissenting view must be wrong. No one wants to be the naysayer who destroys team unity. Finally, each person is happy to be part of the group. Expressing reservations could mean exclusion from it. In our evolutionary past, such banishment guaranteed death; hence our strong urge to remain in the group's favour.

The business world is no stranger to *groupthink*. A classic example is the fate of the world-class airline Swissair. Here, a group of highly paid consultants rallied around the former CEO and, bolstered by the euphoria of past successes, developed a high-risk expansion strategy (including the acquisition of several European airlines). The zealous team built up such a strong consensus that even rational reservations were suppressed, leading to the airline's collapse in 2001.

If you ever find yourself in a tight, unanimous group, you must speak your mind, even if your team does not like it. Question tacit assumptions, even if you risk expulsion from the warm nest. And, if you lead a group, appoint someone as devil's advocate. She will not be the most popular member of the team, but she might be the most important.

See also **Social Proof** (ch. 4); **Social Loafing** (ch. 33); **In-Group Out-Group Bias** (ch. 79); **Planning Fallacy** (ch. 91)

26

WHY YOU'LL SOON BE PLAYING MEGATRILLIONS

Neglect of Probability

Two games of chance: in the first, you can win $10 million, and in the second, $10,000. Which do you play? If you win the first game, it changes your life completely: you can quit your job, tell your boss where to go and live off the winnings. If you hit the jackpot in the second game, you can take a nice vacation in the Caribbean, but you'll be back at your desk quick enough to see your postcard arrive. The probability of winning is one in 100 million in the first game, and one in 10,000 in the second game. So which do you choose?

Our emotions draw us to the first game, even though the second is ten times better, objectively considered (expected win times probability). Therefore, the trend is towards ever-larger jackpots – Mega Millions, Mega Billions, Mega Trillions – no matter how small the odds are.

In a classic experiment from 1972, participants were divided into two groups. The members of the first group were told that they would receive a small electric shock. In the second group, subjects were told that the risk of this happening was only 50%. The researchers measured physical anxiety (heart rate, nervousness, sweating, etc.) shortly before commencing. The result were, well, shocking: there was absolutely no difference. Participants in both groups were equally stressed. Next, the researchers announced a series of reductions in the probability of a shock for the second group: from 50% to 20%, then 10%, then 5%. The result: still no difference! However, when they declared they would increase the *strength* of the expected current, both groups' anxiety levels rose – again, by the same degree. This illustrates that we respond to the expected *magnitude* of an event (the size of the jackpot or the amount of electricity), but not to its *likelihood*. In other words: we lack an intuitive grasp of probability.

The proper term for this is *neglect of probability,* and it leads to errors in decision-making. We invest in start-ups because the potential profit makes dollar signs flash before our eyes, but we forget (or are too lazy) to investigate the slim chances of new businesses actually achieving such growth. Similarly, following extensive media coverage of a plane crash, we cancel flights without really considering the minuscule probability of crashing (which, of course, remains the same before and after such a disaster). Many amateur investors compare their investments solely on the basis of yield. For them, Google shares with a return of 20% must be twice as good as property that returns 10%. That's wrong. It would be a lot smarter to also consider both investments' risks. But then again, we have no natural feel for this so we often turn a blind eye to it.

Back to the experiment with the electric shocks: in group B, the probability of getting a jolt was further reduced: from 5% to 4% to 3%. Only when the probability reached zero did group B respond differently to group A. To us, 0% risk seems infinitely better than a (highly improbable) 1% risk.

To test this, let's examine two methods of treating drinking water. Suppose a river has two equally large tributaries. One is treated using method A, which reduces the risk of dying from contaminated water from 5% to 2%. The other is treated using method B, which reduces the risk from 1% to 0%, i.e. the threat is completely eliminated. So, method A or B? If you think like most people, you will opt for method B – which is silly because with measure A, 3% fewer people die, and with B, just 1% fewer. Method A is three times as good! This fallacy is called the *zero-risk bias*.

A classic example of this is the U.S. Food Act of 1958, which prohibits food that contains cancer-causing substances. Instituted to achieve zero risk of cancer, this ban sounds good at first, but it ended up leading to the use of more dangerous (but non-carcinogenic) food additives. It is also absurd: as Paracelsus illustrated in the sixteenth century, poisoning is always a question of dosage. Furthermore, this law can never be enforced properly since it is impossible to remove the last 'banned' molecule from food. Each farm would have to function like a hyper-sterile computer-chip factory, and the cost of food would increase a hundredfold. Economically, zero risk rarely makes sense. One exception is when the consequences are colossal, such as a deadly, highly contagious virus escaping from a biotech laboratory.

We have no intuitive grasp of risk and thus distinguish poorly between different threats. The more serious the threat and the more emotional the topic (such as radioactivity), the less reassuring a reduction in risk seems to us. Two researchers at the University of Chicago have shown that people are equally afraid of a 99% chance as they are of a 1% chance of contamination by toxic chemicals. An irrational response, but a common one.

See also **Availability Bias** (ch. 11); **Base-Rate Neglect** (ch. 28); **Problem with Averages** (ch. 55); **Survivorship Bias** (ch. 1); **Illusion of Control** (ch. 17); **Exponential Growth** (ch. 34); **Ambiguity Aversion** (ch. 80)

27

WHY THE LAST COOKIE IN THE JAR MAKES YOUR MOUTH WATER

Scarcity Error

Coffee at a friend's house. We sat trying to make conversation while her three children grappled with one another on the floor. Suddenly I remembered that I had brought some glass marbles with me – a whole bag full. I spilled them out on the floor, in the hope that the little angels would play with them in peace. Far from it: a heated argument ensued. I didn't understand what was happening until I looked more closely. Among the countless marbles there was just one blue one, and the children scrambled for it. All the marbles were exactly the same size and shiny and bright. But the blue one had an advantage over the others – it was one of a kind. I had to laugh at how childish children are!

In August 2005, when I heard that Google would launch its own email service, I was dead set on getting an account. (In the end I did.) At the time, new accounts were very restricted and were given out only on invitation. This made me want one even more. But why? Certainly not because I needed another email account (back then, I already had four), nor because Gmail was better than the competition, but simply because not everyone had access to it. Looking back, I have to laugh at how childish adults are!

Rara sunt cara, said the Romans. Rare is valuable. In fact, the *scarcity error* is as old as mankind. My friend with the three children is a part-time real-estate agent. Whenever she has an interested buyer who cannot decide, she calls and says 'A doctor from London saw the plot of land yesterday. He liked it a lot. What about you? Are you still interested?' The doctor from London – sometimes it's a professor or a banker – is, of course, fictitious. The effect is very real, though: it causes prospects to see the opportunity disappearing before their eyes, so they act and close the deal. Why? This is the potential shortage of supply, yet again. Objectively, this situation is incomprehensible: either the prospect wants the land for the set price or he does not – regardless of any doctors from London.

To assess the quality of cookies, Professor Stephen Worchel split participants into two groups. The first group received an entire box of cookies, and the second group just two. In the end, the subjects with just two cookies rated the quality much higher than the first group did. The experiment was repeated several times and always showed the same result.

'Only while stocks last,' the adverts alert. 'Today only,' warn the posters. Gallery owners take advantage of the *scarcity error* by placing red 'sold' dots under most of their paintings, transforming the remaining few works into rare items that must be snatched up quickly. We collect stamps, coins, vintage cars even when they serve no practical purpose. The post office doesn't accept the old stamps, the banks don't take old coins, and the vintage cars are no longer allowed on the road. These are all side issues; the attraction is that they are in short supply.

In one study, students were asked to arrange ten posters in order of attractiveness – with the agreement that afterward they could keep one poster as a reward for their participation. Five minutes later, they were told that the poster with the third highest rating was no longer available. Then they were asked to judge all ten from scratch. The poster that was no longer available was suddenly classified as the most beautiful. In psychology, this phenomenon is called *reactance*: when we are deprived of an option, we suddenly deem it more attractive. It is a kind of act of defiance. It is also known as the *Romeo and Juliet effect*: because the love between the tragic Shakespearean teenagers is forbidden, it knows no bounds. This yearning does not necessarily have to be a romantic one; in the U.S., student parties are often littered with desperately drunk teenagers – just because it's illegal to drink below the age of 21.

In conclusion: the typical response to scarcity is a lapse in clear thinking. Assess products and services solely on the basis of their price and benefits. It should be of no importance if an item is disappearing fast, nor if any doctors from London take an interest.

See also **Contrast Effect** (ch. 10); **Fear of Regret** (ch. 82); **House-Money Effect** (ch. 84)

28

WHEN YOU HEAR HOOFBEATS, DON'T EXPECT A ZEBRA

Base-Rate Neglect

Mark is a thin man from Germany with glasses who likes to listen to Mozart. Which is more likely? That Mark is A) a truck driver or B) a professor of literature in Frankfurt. Most will bet on B, which is wrong. Germany has 10,000 times more truck drivers than Frankfurt has literature professors. Therefore, it is more likely that Mark is a truck driver. So what just happened? The detailed description enticed us to overlook the statistical reality. Scientists call this fallacy *base-rate neglect*: a disregard of fundamental distribution levels. It is one of the most common errors in reasoning. Virtually all journalists, economists and politicians fall for it on a regular basis.

Here is a second example: a young man is stabbed and fatally injured. Which of these is more likely? A) The attacker is a Russian immigrant and imports combat knives illegally, or B) the attacker is a middle-class American. You know the drill now: option B is much more likely because there are a million times more middle-class Americans than there are Russian knife importers.

In medicine, *base-rate neglect* plays an important role. For example, migraines can point (among others) to a viral infection or a brain tumour. However, viral infections are much more common (in other words, they have a higher base rate), so doctors assess patients for these first before testing for tumours. This is very reasonable. In medical school, residents spend a lot of time purging *base-rate neglect*. The motto drummed into any prospective doctor in the United States is: 'When you hear hoofbeats behind you, don't expect to see a zebra.' Which means: investigate the most likely ailments before you start diagnosing exotic diseases, even if you are a specialist in that.

Doctors are the only professionals who enjoy this base-rate training. Regrettably, few people in business are exposed to it. Now and then I see high-flying entrepreneurs' business plans and get very excited by their products, ideas and personalities. I often catch myself thinking: this could be the next Google! But a glance at the base rate brings me back down to earth. The probability that a firm will survive the first five years is 20%. So what then is the probability that they will grow into a global corporation? Almost zero. Warren Buffett once explained why he does not invest in biotech companies: 'How many of these companies make a turnover of several hundred million dollars? It simply does not happen . . . The most likely scenario is that these firms will just hover somewhere in the middle.' This is clear base-rate thinking. For most people, *survivorship bias* (chapter 1) is one of the causes for their *base-rate neglect*. They tend to see only the successful individuals and companies, because the unsuccessful cases are not reported (or are under-reported). This makes them neglect the large part of the 'invisible' cases.

Imagine you are sampling wine in a restaurant and have to guess from which country it comes. The label of the bottle is covered. If, like me, you are not a wine connoisseur, the only lifeline you have is the base rate. You know from experience that about three-quarters of the wines on the menu are of French origin, so reasonably, you guess France, even if you suspect a Chilean or Californian twist.

Sometimes I have the dubious honour of speaking in front of students of elite business schools. When I ask them about their career prospects, most answer that in the medium term, they see themselves on the boards of global companies. Years ago, both my fellow students and I gave the same answer. The way I see it, my role is to give students a base-rate crash course: 'With a degree from this school, the chance of you landing a spot on the board of a Fortune 500 company is less than 0.1%. No matter how smart and ambitious you are, the most likely scenario is that you will end up in middle management.' With this, I earn shocked looks, and tell myself that I have made a small contribution toward mitigating their future mid-life crises.

See also **Survivorship Bias** (ch. 1); **Neglect of Probability** (ch. 26); **Gambler's Fallacy** (ch. 29); **Conjunction Fallacy** (ch. 41); **The Problem with Averages** (ch. 55); **Information Bias** (ch. 59); **Ambiguity Aversion** (ch. 80)

29

WHY THE 'BALANCING FORCE OF THE UNIVERSE' IS BALONEY

Gambler's Fallacy

In the summer of 1913, something incredible happened in Monte Carlo. Crowds gathered around a roulette table and could not believe their eyes. The ball had landed on black twenty times in a row. Many players took advantage of the opportunity and immediately put their money on red. But the ball continued to come to rest on black. Even more people flocked to the table to bet on red. It had to change eventually! But it was black yet again – and again and again. It was not until the twenty-seventh spin that the ball eventually landed on red. By that time, the players had bet millions on the table. In a few spins of the wheel, they were bankrupt.

The average IQ of pupils in a big city is 100. To investigate this, you take a random sample of 50 students. The first child tested has an IQ of 150. What will the average IQ of your 50 students be? Most people guess 100. Somehow, they think that the super-smart student will be balanced out – perhaps by a dismal student with an IQ of 50 or by two below-average students with IQs of 75. But with such a small sample, that is very unlikely. We must expect that the remaining 49 students will represent the average of the population, so they will each have an average IQ of 100.

Forty-nine times 100 plus one IQ of 150 gives us an average of 101 in the sample.

The Monte Carlo example and the IQ experiment show that people believe in the 'balancing force of the universe'. This is the *gambler's fallacy*. However, with independent events, there is no harmonising force at work: a ball cannot remember how many times it has landed on black. Despite this, one of my friends enters the weekly Mega Millions numbers into a spreadsheet, and then plays those that have appeared the least. All this work is for naught. He is another victim of the *gambler's fallacy*.

The following joke illustrates this phenomenon: a mathematician is afraid of flying due to the small risk of a terrorist attack. So, on every flight he takes a bomb with him in his hand luggage. 'The probability of having a bomb on the plane is very low,' he reasons, 'and the probability of having two bombs on the same plane is virtually zero!'

A coin is flipped three times and lands on heads on each occasion. Suppose someone forces you to spend thousands of dollars of your own money betting on the next toss. Would you bet on heads or tails? If you think like most people, you will choose tails, although heads is just as likely. The *gambler's fallacy* leads us to believe that something must change.

A coin is tossed 50 times, and each time it lands on heads. Again, with someone forcing you to bet, do you pick heads or tails? Now that you've seen an example or two, you're wise to the game: you know that it could go either way. But we've just come across another pitfall: the classic *déformation professionnelle* (professional oversight) of mathematicians: common sense would tell you that heads is the wiser choice, since the coin is obviously loaded.

Previously, we looked at *regression to mean*. An example: if you are experiencing record cold where you live, it is likely that the temperature will return to normal values over the next few days. If the weather functioned like a casino, there would be a 50% chance that the temperature would rise and a 50% chance that it would drop. But the weather is not like a casino. Complex feedback mechanisms in the atmosphere ensure that extremes balance themselves out. In other cases, however, extremes intensify. For example, the rich tend to get richer. A stock that shoots up creates its own demand to a certain extent, simply because it stands out so much – a sort of reverse compensation effect.

So, take a closer look at the independent and interdependent events around you. Purely independent events really only exist at the casino, in the lottery and in theory. In real life, in the financial markets and in business, with the weather and your health, events are often interrelated. What has already happened has an influence on what will happen. As comforting an idea as it is, there is simply no balancing force out there for independent events. 'What goes around, comes around' simply does not exist.

See also **Problem with Averages** (ch. 55); **Base-Rate Neglect** (ch. 28); **Déformation Professionnelle** (ch. 92); **Regression to the Mean** (ch. 19); **Simple Logic** (ch. 63)

30

WHY THE WHEEL OF FORTUNE MAKES OUR HEADS SPIN

The Anchor

When was Abraham Lincoln born? If you don't know the year off the top of your head, and your smartphone battery has just died, how do you answer this? Perhaps you know that he was president during the Civil War in the 1860s and that he was the first U.S. president to be assassinated. Looking at the Lincoln Memorial in Washington, you don't see a young, energetic man but something more akin to a worn-out 60-year-old veteran. The memorial must depict him at the height of his political power, say at the age of 60. Let's assume that he was assassinated in the mid-1860s, making 1805 our estimate for the year he was born. (The correct answer is 1809.) So how did we work it out? We found an *anchor* to help us – the 1860s – and worked from there to an educated guess.

Whenever we have to guess something – the length of the Mississippi River, population density in Russia, the number of nuclear power plants in France – we use *anchors*. We start with something we are sure of and venture into unfamiliar territory from there. How else could we do it? Just pick a number off the top of our heads? That would be irrational.

Unfortunately, we also use *anchors* when we don't need to. For example, one day in a lecture, a professor placed a bottle of wine on the table. He asked his students to write down the last two digits of their social security numbers and then decide if they would be willing to spend that amount on the wine. In the auction that followed, students with higher numbers bid nearly twice as much as students with lower numbers. The social security digits worked as an *anchor* – albeit in a hidden and misleading way.

The psychologist Amos Tversky conducted an experiment involving a wheel of fortune. He had participants spin it, and afterward, they were asked how many member states the United Nations has. Their guesses confirmed the *anchor* effect: the highest estimates came from people who had spun high numbers on the wheel.

Researchers Russo and Shoemaker asked students in what year Attila the Hun suffered his crushing defeat in Europe. Just like the example with social security numbers, the participants were anchored – this time with the last few digits of their telephone number. The result? People with higher numbers chose later years and vice versa. (If you were wondering, Attila's demise came about in 453.)

Another experiment: students and professional real-estate agents were given a tour of a house and asked to estimate its value. Beforehand, they were informed about a (randomly generated) listed sales price. As might be expected, the *anchor* influenced the students: the higher this price, the higher they valued the property. And the professionals? Did they value the house objectively? No, they were similarly influenced by the random *anchor* amount. The more uncertain the value of something – such as real estate, company stock or art – the more susceptible even experts are to *anchors*.

Anchors abound, and we all clutch at them. The 'recommended retail price' printed on many products is nothing more than an *anchor*. Sales professionals know they must establish a price at an early stage – long before they have an offer. Also, it has been proven that if teachers know students' past grades, it influences how they will mark new work. The most recent grades act as a starting point.

In my early years, I had a quick stint at a consulting firm. My boss was a pro when it came to using *anchors*. In his first conversation with any client, he made sure to fix an opening price, which, by the way, almost criminally exceeded our internal costs: 'I'll tell you this now so you're not surprised when you receive the quote, Mr. So-and-So: we've just completed a similar project for one of your competitors and it was in the range of five million dollars.' The *anchor* was dropped: the price negotiations started at exactly five million.

See also **Framing** (ch. 42)

31

HOW TO RELIEVE PEOPLE OF THEIR MILLIONS

Induction

A farmer feeds a goose. At first, the shy animal is hesitant, wondering 'What's going on here? Why is he feeding me?' This continues for a few more weeks until, eventually, the goose's scepticism gives way. After a few months, the goose is sure that 'The farmer has my best interests at heart.' Each additional day's feeding confirms this. Fully convinced of the man's benevolence, the goose is amazed when he takes it out of its enclosure on Christmas Day – and slaughters it. The Christmas goose fell victim to *inductive thinking*, the inclination to draw universal certainties from individual observations. Philosopher David Hume used this allegory back in the eighteenth century to warn of its pitfalls. However, it's not just geese that are susceptible to it.

An investor buys shares in stock X. The share price rockets, and at first he is wary. 'Probably a bubble,' he suspects. As the stock continues to rise, even after months, his apprehension turns into excitement: 'This stock may never come down' – especially since every day this is the case. After half a year, he invests his life savings in it, turning a blind eye to the huge cluster risk this poses. Later, the man will pay for his foolish investment. He has fallen hook, line and sinker for *induction*.

Inductive thinking doesn't have to be a road to ruin, though. In fact, you can make a fortune with it by sending a few emails. Here's how Nassim Taleb describes it (although with fewer addresses): put together two stock market forecasts – one predicting that prices will rise next month and one warning of a drop. Send the first email to 50,000 people, and the second email to a different set of 50,000. Suppose that after one month, the indices have fallen. Now you can send another email, but this time only to the 50,000 people who received a correct prediction. These 50,000 you divide into two groups: the first half learns that prices will increase next month, the second half discovers they will fall. Continue doing this. After 10 months, around 100 people will remain, all of whom you have advised impeccably. From their perspective, you are a genius. You have proven that you are truly in possession of prophetic powers. Some of these people will trust you with their money. Take it and start a new life in Brazil. Taleb describes this trick in *Fooled by Randomness*, however, with only 10,000 names.

However, it's not just naïve strangers who get deceived in this way; we constantly trick ourselves, too. For example, people who are rarely ill consider themselves immortal. CEOs who announce increased profits in consecutive quarters deem themselves infallible – their employees and shareholders do, too. I once had a friend who was a base jumper. He jumped off cliffs, antennae, and buildings, pulling the ripcord only at the last minute. One day, I brought up how risky his chosen sport is. He replied quite matter-of-factly: 'I've over 1,000 jumps under my belt, and nothing has ever happened to me.' Two months later, he was dead. It happened when he jumped from a particularly dangerous

cliff in South Africa. This single event was enough to erad-
icate a theory confirmed a thousand times over.

Inductive thinking can have devastating results. Yet we
cannot do without it. We trust that, when we board a plane,
aerodynamic laws will still be valid. We imagine that we
will not be randomly beaten up on the street. We expect
that our hearts will still be beating tomorrow. These are
confidences without which we could not live, but we must
remember that certainties are always provisional. As
Benjamin Franklin said, 'Nothing is certain but death and
taxes.'

Induction seduces us and leads us to conclusions such
as: 'Mankind has always survived, so we will be able to
tackle any future challenges, too.' Sounds good in theory,
but what we fail to realise is that such a statement can only
come from a species that has lasted until now. To assume
that our existence to date is an indication of our future
survival is a serious flaw in reasoning. Probably the most
serious of all.

See also **False Causality** (ch.37); **Survivorship Bias** (ch. 1)

32

WHY EVIL STRIKES HARDER THAN GOOD

Loss Aversion

On a scale of 1 to 10, how good do you feel today? Now consider what would bring you up to a perfect 10. That vacation in the Caribbean you've always dreamed of? A step up the career ladder maybe? Next question: what would make you drop down by the same number of points? Paralysis, Alzheimer's, cancer, depression, war, hunger, torture, financial ruin, damage to your reputation, losing your best friend, your children getting kidnapped, blindness, death? The long list of possibilities makes us realise just how many obstacles to happiness exist; in short, there are more bad things than good – and they are far more consequential.

In our evolutionary past, this was even more the case. One stupid mistake and you were dead. Everything could lead to your rapid departure from the game of life – carelessness on the hunt, an inflamed tendon, exclusion from the group and so on. People who were reckless or gung-ho died before they could pass their genes on to the next generation. Those who remained, the cautious, survived. We are their descendants.

So, no wonder we fear loss more than we value gain. Losing $100 costs you a greater amount of happiness than the delight you would feel if I gave you $100. In fact, it has been proven that, emotionally, a loss 'weighs' about twice that of a similar gain. Social scientists call this *loss aversion*.

For this reason, if you want to convince someone about something, don't focus on the advantages; instead highlight how it helps them dodge the disadvantages. Here is an example from a campaign promoting breast self-examination (BSE): two different leaflets were handed out to women. Pamphlet A urged: 'Research shows that women who *do* BSE have an *increased* chance of finding a tumour in the early, more treatable state of the disease.' Pamphlet B said: 'Research shows that women who do *not do* BSE have a *decreased* chance of finding a tumour in the early, more treatable state of the disease.' The study revealed that pamphlet B (written in a 'loss-frame') generated significantly more awareness and BSE behaviour than pamphlet A (written in a 'gain-frame').

The fear of losing something motivates people more than the prospect of gaining something of equal value. Suppose your business is home insulation. The most effective way of encouraging customers to purchase your product is to tell them how much money they are losing without insulation – as opposed to how much money they would save with it, even though the amount is exactly the same.

This type of aversion is also found on the stock market, where investors tend to simply ignore losses on paper. After all, an unrealised loss isn't as painful as a realised one. So they sit on the stock, even if the chance of recovery is small and the probability of further decline is large. I once met a man, a multimillionaire, who was terribly upset because he had lost a $100 bill. What a waste of emotion! I pointed out that the value of his portfolio fluctuated by at least $100 every second.

Management gurus push employees in large companies to be bolder and more entrepreneurial. The reality is: employees tend to be risk-averse. From their perspective, this aversion makes perfect sense: why risk something that brings them, at best, a nice bonus, and at worst, a pink slip? The downside is larger than the upside. In almost all companies and situations, safeguarding your career trumps any potential reward. So, if you've been scratching your head about the lack of risk-taking among your employees, you now know why. (However, if employees do take big risks, it is often when they can hide behind group decisions. Learn more in chapter 33 on *social loafing*.)

We can't fight it: evil is more powerful and more plentiful than good. We are more sensitive to negative than to positive things. On the street, scary faces stand out more than smiling ones. We remember bad behaviour longer than good – except, of course, when it comes to ourselves.

See also **House-Money Effect** (ch. 84); **Endowment Effect** (ch. 23); **Social Loafing** (ch. 33); **Default Effect** (ch. 81); **Sunk Cost Fallacy** (ch. 5); **Framing** (ch. 42); **Affect Heuristic** (ch. 66)

33

WHY TEAMS ARE LAZY

Social Loafing

In 1913 Maximilian Ringelmann, a French engineer, studied the performance of horses. He concluded that the power of two animals pulling a coach did not equal twice the power of a single horse. Surprised by this result, he extended his research to humans. He had several men pull a rope and measured the force applied by each individual. On average, if two people were pulling together, each invested just 93% of their individual strength, when three pulled together, it was 85%, and with eight people, just 49%.

Science calls this the *social loafing* effect. It occurs when individual performance is not directly visible; it blends in to the group effort. It occurs among rowers, but not in relay races, because here, individual contributions are evident. *Social loafing* is rational behaviour: why invest all of your energy when half will do – especially when this little shortcut goes unnoticed? Quite simply, *social loafing* is a form of cheating of which we are all guilty even if it takes place unconsciously, just as it did with Ringelmann's horses.

When people work together, individual performances decrease. This isn't surprising. What is noteworthy, however, is that our input doesn't grind to a complete halt. So what stops us from putting our feet up completely and letting the others do all the hard work? The consequences.

Zero-performance would be noticed, and it brings with it weighty punishments, such as exclusion from the group or vilification. Evolution has led us to develop many fine-tuned senses, including how much idleness we can get away with and how to recognise it in others.

Social loafing does not occur solely in physical performance. We slack off mentally, too. For example, in meetings, the larger the team the weaker our individual participation. However, once a certain number of participants is involved, our performance plateaus. Whether the group consists of 20 or 100 people is not important – maximum inertia has been achieved.

One question remains: who came up with the much-vaunted idea that teams achieve more than individual workers? Maybe the Japanese. Thirty years ago, they flooded global markets with their products. Business economists looked more closely at the industrial miracle and saw that Japanese factories were organised into teams. This model was copied – with mixed success. What worked very well in Japan could not be replicated with the Americans and Europeans – perhaps because *social loafing* rarely happens there. In the West, teams function better if and only if they are small and consist of diverse, specialised people. This makes sense, because within such groups, indi-vidual performances can be traced back to each specialist.

Social loafing has interesting implications. In groups, we tend to hold back not only in terms of participation, but also in terms of accountability. Nobody wants to take the rap for the misdeeds or poor decisions of the whole group. A glaring example is the prosecution of the Nazis at the Nuremberg trials, or less controversially, any board or management team. We hide behind team decisions. The technical term for this is *diffusion of responsibility*. For the same reason, teams tend to take bigger risks than their members would take on their own. The individual group members reason that they are not the only ones who will be blamed if things go wrong. This effect is called *risky shift*, and is especially hazardous among company and pension-fund strategists, where billions are at stake, or in defence departments, where groups decide on the use of nuclear weapons.

In conclusion: people behave differently in groups than when alone (otherwise there would be no groups). The disadvantages of groups can be mitigated by making individual performances as visible as possible. Long live meritocracy! Long live the performance society!

See also **Motivation Crowding** (ch. 56); **Social Proof** (ch. 4); **Groupthink** (ch. 25); **Loss Aversion** (ch. 32)

34

STUMPED BY A SHEET OF PAPER

Exponential Growth

A piece of paper is folded in two, then in half again, again and again. How thick will it be after 50 folds? Write down your guess before you continue reading.

Second task. Choose between these options: A) Over the next 30 days, I will give you $1,000 a day. B) Over the next 30 days, I will give you a cent on the first day, two cents on the second day, four cents on the third day, eight cents on the fourth day, and so on. Don't think too long about it: A or B?

Are you ready? Well, if we assume that a sheet of copy paper is approximately 0.004 inches thick, then its thickness after 50 folds is a little over 70 million miles. This equals the distance between the earth and the sun, as you can check easily with a calculator. With the second question, it is worthwhile choosing option B, even though A sounds more tempting. Selecting A earns you $30,000 in 30 days; choosing B gives you more than $10 million.

Linear growth we understand intuitively. However, we have no sense of exponential (or percentage) growth. Why is this? Because we didn't need it before. Our ancestors' experiences were mostly of the linear variety. Whoever spent twice the time collecting berries earned double the amount. Whoever hunted two mammoths instead of one could eat for twice as long. In the Stone Age, people rarely came across *exponential growth*. Today, things are different.

'Each year, the number of traffic accidents rises by 7%,' warns a politician. Let's be honest: we don't intuitively understand what this means. So, let's use a trick and calculate the 'doubling time'. Start with the magic number of 70 and divide it by the growth rate in per cent. In this instance: 70 divided by 7 = 10 years. So what the politician is saying is: 'The number of traffic accidents doubles every 10 years.' Pretty alarming. (You may ask: 'Why the number 70?' This has to do with a mathematical concept called logarithm. You can look it up in the notes section.)

Another example: 'Inflation is at 5%.' Whoever hears this thinks: 'That's not so bad, what's 5% anyway?' Let's quickly calculate the doubling time: 70 divided by 5 = 14 years. In 14 years, a dollar will be worth only half what it is today – a catastrophe for anyone who has a savings account.

Suppose you are a journalist and learn that the number of registered dogs in your city is rising by 10% a year. Which headline do you put on your article? Certainly not: 'Dog registrations increasing by 10%.' No one will care. Instead, announce: 'Deluge of dogs: twice as many mutts in 7 years' time!'

Nothing that grows exponentially grows for ever. Most politicians, economists and journalists forget that. Such growth will eventually reach a limit. Guaranteed. For example, the intestinal bacterium, Escherichia coli, divides every twenty minutes. In just a few days it could cover the whole planet, but since it consumes more oxygen and sugar than is available, its growth has a cut-off point.

The ancient Persians were well aware that people struggled with percentage growth. Here is a local tale: there was once a wise courtier, who presented the king with a chessboard. Moved by the gift, the king said to him: 'Tell me how I can thank you.' The courtier replied: 'Your Highness, I want nothing more than for you to cover the chessboard with rice, putting one grain of rice on the first square, and then on every subsequent square, twice the previous number of grains.' The king was astonished: 'It is an honour to you, dear courtier, that you present such a modest request.'

But how much rice is that? The king guessed about a sack. Only when his servants began the task – placing a grain on the first square, two grains of rice on the second square, four grains of rice on the third, and so on – did he realise that he would need more rice than was growing on earth.

When it comes to growth rates, do not trust your intuition. You don't have any. Accept it. What really helps is a calculator, or, with low growth rates, the magic number of 70.

See also **Simple Logic** (ch. 63); **Neglect of Probability** (ch. 26); **The Law of Small Numbers** (ch. 61)

35

CURB YOUR ENTHUSIASM

Winner's Curse

Texas in the 1950s. A piece of land is being auctioned. Ten oil companies are vying for it. Each has made an estimate of how much the site is worth. The lowest assessment is $10 million, and the highest is $100 million. The higher the price climbs during the auction, the more firms exit the bidding. Finally, one company submits the highest bid and wins. Champagne corks pop.

The *winner's curse* suggests that the winner of an auction often turns out to be the loser. Industry analysts have noted that companies that regularly emerged as winning bidders from these oilfield auctions systematically paid too much, and years later went under. This is understandable. If the estimates vary between $10 million and $100 million, the actual value most likely lies somewhere in the middle. The highest bid at an auction is often much too high – unless these bidders have critical information others are not privy to. This was not the case in Texas. The oil managers actually celebrated a Pyrrhic victory.

Today, this phenomenon affects us all. From eBay to Groupon to Google AdWords, prices are consistently set by auction. Bidding wars for cellphone frequencies drive telecom companies to the brink of bankruptcy. Airports rent out their commercial spaces to the highest bidder. And if

Walmart plans to introduce a new detergent and asks for tenders from five suppliers, that's nothing more than an auction – with the risk of the *winner's curse*.

The auctioning of everyday life has now reached tradesmen, too, thanks to the Internet. When my walls needed a new lick of paint, instead of tracking down the handiest painter, I advertised the job online. Thirty painters, some from more than 300 miles away, competed for the job. The best offer was so low that, out of compassion, I could not accept it – to spare the poor painter the *winner's curse*.

Initial Public Offerings (IPOs) are also examples of auctions. And, when companies buy other companies – the infamous mergers and acquisitions – the *winner's curse* is present more often than not. Astoundingly, more than half of all acquisitions destroy value, according to a McKinsey study.

So why do we fall victim to the *winner's curse*? First, the real value of many things is uncertain. Additionally, the more interested parties, the greater the likelihood of an overly enthusiastic bid. Second, we want to outdo competitors. A friend owns a micro-antenna factory and told me about the cut-throat bidding war that Apple instigated during the development of the iPhone. Everyone wants to be the official supplier to Apple even though whoever gets the contract is likely to lose money.

So how much would you pay for $100? Imagine that you and an opponent are invited to take part in such an auction. The rules: whoever makes the highest offer gets the $100 bill, and – most importantly – when this happens, both bidders have to pay their final offer. How high will you go? From your perspective, it makes sense to pay $20, $30 or $40. Your opponent does the same. Even $99 seems like a reasonable offer for a $100 bill. Now, your competitor offers $100. If this remains the highest bid, he will come away breaking even (paying $100 for $100), whereas you will simply have to cough up $99. So you continue to bid. At $110, you have a guaranteed loss of $10, but your opponent would have to shell out $109 (his last bid). So he will continue playing. When do you stop? When will your competitor give up? Try it out with friends.

In conclusion: accept this piece of wisdom about auctions from Warren Buffett: 'Don't go.' If you happen to work in an industry where they are inevitable, set a maximum price and deduct 20% from this to offset the *winner's curse*. Write this number on a piece of paper and don't go a cent over it.

See also **Endowment Effect** (ch. 23)

36

NEVER ASK A WRITER IF THE NOVEL IS AUTOBIOGRAPHICAL

Fundamental Attribution Error

Opening the newspaper, you learn that another CEO has been forced to step down because of bad results. In the sports section, you read that your team's winning season was thanks to player X or coach Y. In history books, you learn that the success of the French army in the early 1800s is a testament to Napoleon's superb leadership and strategy. 'Every story has a face', it seems. Indeed this is an ironclad rule in every newsroom. Always on the lookout for the 'people angle', journalists (and their readers) take this principle one step further, and thus fall prey to the *fundamental attribution error*. This describes the tendency to overestimate individuals' influence and underestimate external, situational factors.

In 1967, researchers at Duke University set up the following experiment: participants read an argument either lauding or vilifying Fidel Castro. They were informed that the author of the text had been allocated the viewpoint regardless of his true political views; he was just making a coherent argument. Nevertheless, most of the audience believed what he said reflected his true opinion. They falsely attributed the content of the speech to his character, and ignored the external factors; in this case the professors who had crafted the text.

The *fundamental attribution error* is particularly useful

for whittling negative events into neat little packages. For example, the 'blame' for wars we lazily push on to individuals: the Yugoslav assassin in Sarajevo has World War I on his conscience, and Hitler singlehandedly caused World War II. Many swallow these simplifications, even though wars are unforeseeable events whose innumerable dynamics we may never fully understand. Which sounds a little like financial markets and climate issues, don't you agree?

We see this same pattern when companies announce good or bad results. All eyes shift to the CEO's office, even if we know the truth: economic success depends far more on the overall economic climate and the industry's attractiveness than on brilliant leadership. It is interesting how frequently firms in ailing industries replace their CEOs – and how seldom that happens in booming sectors. Are ailing industries less careful in their recruitment processes? Such decisions are no more rational than what happens between football coaches and their clubs.

I often go to musical concerts. In my home town of Lucerne, in the centre of Switzerland, I am spoiled with one-off classical recitals. During the intermission, however, I notice that the conversations almost always revolve around the conductors and/or soloists. With the exception of world premieres, composition is rarely discussed. Why? The real miracle of music is, after all, the composition: the creation of sounds, moods and rhythms where previously only a blank sheet lay. The difference among scores is a thousand times more impressive than the difference among performances of the same score. But we do not think like this. The score is – in contrast to the conductors and soloists – faceless.

In my career as a fiction writer, I experience the

fundamental attribution error in this way: after a reading (which in itself is a debatable undertaking), the first question always, really always, is: 'What part of your novel is autobiographical?' I often feel like thundering: 'It's not about me, damn it! It's about the book, the text, the language, the credibility of the story!' But unfortunately my upbringing allows such outbursts only rarely.

We shouldn't judge those guilty of the *fundamental attribution error* too harshly. Our preoccupation with other people stems from our evolutionary past: belonging to a group was necessary for survival. Reproduction, defence, and hunting large animals – all these were impossible tasks for individuals to achieve alone. Banishment meant certain death, and those who actively opted for the solitary life – of whom there were surely a few – fared no better and also disappeared from the gene pool. In short, our lives depended on and revolved around others, which explains why we are so obsessed with our fellow humans today. The result of this infatuation is that we spend about 90% of our time thinking about other people, and dedicate just 10% to assessing other factors and contexts.

In conclusion: as much as we are fascinated by the spectacle of life, the people on stage are not perfect, self-governed individuals. Instead they tumble from situation to situation. If you want to understand the current play – really understand it – then forget about the performers. Pay close attention to the dance of influences to which the actors are subjected.

See also **Story Bias** (ch. 13); **Swimmer's Body Illusion** (ch. 2); **Salience Effect** (ch. 83); **News Illusion** (ch. 99); **Halo Effect** (ch. 38); **Fallacy of the Single Cause** (ch. 97)

37

WHY YOU SHOULDN'T BELIEVE IN THE STORK

False Causality

For the inhabitants of the Hebrides, a chain of islands north of Scotland, head lice were a part of life. If the lice left their host, he became sick and feverish. Therefore, to dispel the fever, sick people had lice put in their hair intentionally. There was a method to their madness: as soon as the lice had settled in again, the patient improved.

In one city, a study revealed that in each blaze, the more firefighters called out to fight it the greater the fire damage. The mayor imposed an immediate hiring freeze and cut the firefighting budget.

Both stories come from German physics professors Hans-Peter Beck-Bornholdt and Hans-Hermann Dubben. In their book (unfortunately there is no English version), they illustrate the muddling of cause and effect. If the lice leave the invalid, it is because he has a fever and they simply get hot feet. When the fever breaks, they return. And the bigger the blaze, the more firefighters were called out – not, of course, vice versa.

We may smirk at these stories, but *false causality* leads us astray practically every day. Consider the headline 'Employee motivation leads to higher corporate profits.' Does it? Maybe people are simply more motivated because the company is doing well. Another headline touts that the more women on a corporate board, the more profitable the firm is. But is that really how it works? Or do highly profitable firms simply tend to recruit more women to their boards? Business-book authors and consultants often operate with similar false – or at least fuzzy – causalities.

In the 90s, there was no one holier than the then head of the Federal Reserve, Alan Greenspan. His obscure remarks gave monetary policy the aura of a secret science that kept the country on the secure path of prosperity. Politicians, journalists and business leaders idolised Greenspan. Today we know that these commentators fell victim to *false causality*. America's symbiosis with China, the globe's low-cost producer and eager buyer of U.S. debt, played a much more important role. In other words, Greenspan was simply lucky that the economy did so well during his tenure.

A further example: scientists found that long periods in the hospital affected patients adversely. This was music to health insurers' ears; they, of course, are keen to make stays as brief as possible. But, clearly, patients who are discharged immediately are healthier than those who must stay on for treatment. This hardly makes long stays detrimental.

Or, take this headline: 'Fact: Women who use shampoo XYZ every day have stronger hair.' Though the context can be substantiated scientifically, this statement says very little – least of all that the shampoo makes your hair stronger. It might simply be the other way round: women with strong hair tend to use shampoo XYZ – and perhaps that's because it says 'especially for thick hair' on the bottle.

Recently I read that students get better grades at school if their homes contain a lot of books. This study was surely a shot in the arm for booksellers, but it is another fine example of *false causality*. The simple truth is that educated parents tend to value their children's education more than uneducated ones do. Plus, educated parents often have more books at home. In short, a dust-covered copy of *War and Peace* alone isn't going to influence anyone's grades; what counts is parents' education levels, as well as their genes.

The best example of *false causality* was the supposed relationship between the birth rate and the numbers of stork pairs in Germany. Both were in decline, and if you plot them on a graph the two lines of development from 1965 to 1987 appeared almost identical. Does this mean the stork actually does bring babies? Obviously not, since this was a purely coincidental correlation.

In conclusion: correlation is not causality. Take a closer look at linked events: sometimes what is presented as the cause turns out to be the effect, and vice versa. And sometimes there is no link at all – just like with the storks and babies.

See also **Coincidence** (ch. 24); **Association Bias** (ch. 48); **Clustering Illusion** (ch. 3); **Story Bias** (ch. 13); **Induction** (ch. 31); **Beginner's Luck** (ch. 49)

38

EVERYONE IS BEAUTIFUL AT THE TOP

Halo Effect

Cisco, the Silicon Valley firm, was once a darling of the new economy. Business journalists gushed about its success in every discipline: its wonderful customer service, perfect strategy, skilful acquisitions, unique corporate culture and charismatic CEO. In March 2000, it was the most valuable company in the world.

When Cisco's stock plummeted 80% the following year, the journalists changed their tune. Suddenly the company's competitive advantages were reframed as destructive short-comings: poor customer service, a woolly strategy, clumsy acquisitions, a lame corporate culture and an insipid CEO. All this – and yet neither the strategy nor the CEO had changed. What had changed, in the wake of the dot-com crash, was demand for Cisco's product – and that was through no fault of the firm.

The *halo effect* occurs when a single aspect dazzles us and affects how we see the full picture. In the case of Cisco, its halo shone particularly bright. Journalists were astounded by its stock prices and assumed the entire business was just as brilliant – without making closer investigation.

The *halo effect* always works the same way: we take a simple-to-obtain or remarkable fact or detail, such as a company's financial situation, and extrapolate conclusions from there that are harder to nail down, such as the merit of its management or the feasibility of its strategy. We often ascribe success and superiority where little is due, such as when we favour products from a manufacturer simply because of its good reputation. Another example of the *halo effect*: we believe that CEOs who are successful in one industry will thrive in any sector – and furthermore that they are heroes in their private lives, too.

The psychologist Edward Lee Thorndike discovered the *halo effect* nearly 100 years ago. His conclusion was that a single quality (e.g., beauty, social status, age) produces a positive or negative impression that outshines everything else, and the overall effect is disproportionate. Beauty is the best-studied example. Dozens of studies have shown that we automatically regard good-looking people as more pleasant, honest and intelligent. Attractive people also have it easier in their professional lives – and that has nothing to do with the myth of women 'sleeping their way to the top'. The effect can even be detected in schools, where teachers unconsciously give good-looking students better grades.

Advertising has found an ally in the *halo effect*: just look at the number of celebrities smiling at us from TV ads, billboards and magazines. What makes a professional tennis player like Roger Federer a coffee machine expert is still open for debate, but this hasn't detracted from the success of the campaign. We are so used to seeing celebrities promoting arbitrary products that we never stop to consider why their support should be of any importance to us. But this is exactly the sneaky part of the *halo effect*: it works on a subconscious level. All that needs to register is the attractive face, dream lifestyle – and that product.

Sticking with negative effects, the *halo effect* can lead to great injustice and even stereotyping when nationality, gender, or race becomes the all-encompassing feature. One need be neither racist nor sexist to fall victim to this. The *halo effect* clouds our view, just as it does the view of journalists, educators, and consumers.

Occasionally, this effect has pleasant consequences – at least in the short term. Have you ever been head over heels in love? If so, you know how flawless a person can appear. Your Mr or Ms Perfect seems to be the whole package: attractive, intelligent, likeable and warm. Even when your friends might point out obvious failings, you see nothing but endearing quirks.

The *halo effect* obstructs our view of true characteristics. To counteract this, go beyond face value. Factor out the most striking features. World-class orchestras achieve this by making candidates play behind a screen, so that sex, race, age and appearance play no part in their decision. To business journalists I warmly recommend judging a company by something other than its easily obtainable quarterly figures (the stock market already delivers that). Dig deeper. Invest the time to do serious research. What emerges is not always pretty, but almost always educational.

See also **Fundamental Attribution Error** (ch. 36); **Salience Effect** (ch. 83); **Swimmer's Body Illusion** (ch. 2); **Contrast Effect** (ch. 10); **Expectations** (ch. 62)

39

CONGRATULATIONS! YOU'VE WON RUSSIAN ROULETTE

Alternative Paths

You arrange to meet with a Russian oligarch in a forest just outside your city. He arrives shortly after you, carrying a suitcase and a gun. Placing the suitcase on the hood of his car, he opens it so you can see it is filled to the brim with stacks of money – $10 million in total. 'Want to play Russian roulette?' he asks. 'Pull the trigger once, and all this is yours.' The revolver contains a single bullet; the other five chambers are empty. You consider your options. $10 million would change your life. You would never have to work again. You could finally move from collecting stamps to collecting sports cars!

You accept the challenge. You put the revolver to your temple and squeeze the trigger. You hear a faint click and feel adrenaline flood your body. Nothing happens. The chamber was empty! You have survived. You take the money, move to the most beautiful city you know and upset the locals by building a luxurious villa there.

One of these neighbours, whose home now stands in the shadow of yours, is a prominent lawyer. He works twelve hours a day, 300 days a year. His rates are impressive, but not unusual: $500 per hour. Each year he can put aside half a million net after taxes and living expenses. From time to time, you wave to him from your driveway, laughing on the inside: he will have to work for twenty years to catch up with you.

Suppose that, after twenty years, your hard-working neighbour has saved up $10 million. A journalist comes along one day and puts together a piece on the more affluent residents in the area – complete with photos of the magnificent buildings and the beautiful second wives that you and your neighbour have accrued. He comments on the interior design and the exquisite landscaping. However, the crucial difference between the two of you remains hidden from view: the risk that lurks behind each of the $10 million. For this he would need to recognise the *alternative paths*.

But not only journalists are underachievers at this skill. We all are, as Nassim Taleb makes clear with the Russian roulette vignette.

Alternative paths are all the outcomes that could have happened, but did not. With the game of Russian roulette, four *alternative paths* would have led to the same result (winning the $10 million) and the fifth alternative to your death. A huge difference. In the case of the lawyer, the possible paths lie much more close together. In a village, he would have earned perhaps just $200 per hour. In the heart of New York working for one of the major investment banks, maybe it would have been $600 per hour. But, unlike you, he risked no *alternative path* that would have cost him his fortune – or his life.

Alternative paths are invisible, so we contemplate them very rarely. Those who speculate on junk bonds, options and credit default swaps, thus making millions, should never forget that they flirt with many *alternative paths* that lead straight to ruin. To a rational mind, ten million dollars that comes about through a huge risk is worth less than the same sum earned by years of drudgery. (An accountant might disagree, though.)

In *Fooled by Randomness*, Taleb recounts how he had dinner with a friend in a bar in New York. 'We flipped a coin to see who was going to pay for the meal. I lost and paid. He was about to thank me when he abruptly stopped and said that he paid for half of it *probabilistically*.' The friend was considering *alternative paths*.

In conclusion: risk is not directly visible. Therefore, always consider what the *alternative paths* are. Success that comes about through risky dealings is, to a rational mind, of less worth than success achieved the 'boring' way (for example, with laborious work as a lawyer, a dentist, a ski instructor, a pilot, a hairdresser or a consultant). Yes, looking at *alternative paths* from the outside is a difficult task. Looking at them from the inside is an almost impossible task. Your brain will do everything to convince you that your success is warranted – no matter how risky your dealings are – and will obscure any thought of paths other than the one you are on.

See also **Black Swan** (ch. 75); **Ambiguity Aversion** (ch. 80); **Fear of Regret** (ch. 82); **Self-Selection Bias** (ch. 47)

40

FALSE PROPHETS

Forecast Illusion

'Facebook to be number one entertainment platform in
   three years.'
'Regime shift in North Korea in two years.'
'Sour grapes for France as Argentinian wines expected to
   dominate.'
'Euro collapse likely.'
'Low-cost space flights by 2025.'
'No more crude oil in 15 years.'

Every day, experts bombard us with predictions, but how
reliable are they? Until a few years ago, no one bothered to
check. Then along came Philip Tetlock. Over a period of
ten years, he evaluated 28,361 predictions from 284 self-
appointed professionals. The result: in terms of accuracy,
the experts fared only marginally better than a random
forecast generator. Ironically, the media darlings were
among the poorest performers; and of those the worst were
the prophets of doom and disintegration. Examples of
their far-fetched forecasts included the collapse of Canada,
Nigeria, China, India, Indonesia, South Africa, Belgium
and the E.U. None of these countries has imploded.

   'There are two kinds of forecasters: those who don't
know, and those who don't know they don't know,' wrote

Harvard economist John Kenneth Galbraith. With this he made himself a figure of hatred in his own guild. Fund manager Peter Lynch summed it up even more cuttingly: 'There are 60,000 economists in the U.S., many of them employed full-time trying to forecast recessions and interest rates, and if they could do it successfully twice in a row, they'd all be millionaires by now [. . .] As far as I know, most of them are still gainfully employed, which ought to tell us something.' That was ten years ago. Today, the U.S. could employ three times as many economists – with little or no effect on the quality of their forecasts.

The problem is that experts enjoy free rein with few negative consequences. If they strike it lucky, they enjoy publicity, consultancy offers and publication deals. If they are completely off the mark, they face no penalties – either in terms of financial compensation or in loss of reputation. This win-win scenario virtually incentivises them to churn out as many prophecies as they can muster. Indeed, the more forecasts they generate, the more will be coincidentally correct. Ideally, they should have to pay into some sort of 'forecast fund' – say $1,000 per prediction. If the forecast is correct, the expert gets his money back with interest. If he is wrong, the money goes to charity.

So what is predictable and what is not? Some things are fairly simple. For example, I have a rough idea of how many pounds I will weigh in a year's time. However, the more complex a system, and the longer the time frame, the more blurred the view of the future will be. Global warming, oil prices or exchange rates are almost impossible to foresee. Inventions are not at all predictable because if we knew what technology we would invent in the future we would already have invented it.

So, be critical when you encounter predictions. Whenever I hear one, I make sure to smile, no matter how bleak it is. Then I ask myself two questions. First, what incentive does the expert have? If he is an employee, could he lose his job if he is always wrong? Or is he a self-appointed guru who earns a living through books and lectures? The latter type of forecaster relies on the media's attention so, predictably, his prophecies tend to be sensational. Second, how good is his success rate? How many predictions has he made over the past five years? Out of these, how many have been right and how many have not? This information is vital yet often goes unreported. I implore the media: please don't publish any more forecasts without giving the pundit's track record.

Finally, since it is so fitting, a quote from former British prime minister Tony Blair: 'I don't make predictions. I never have, and I never will.'

See also **Expectations** (ch. 62); **Planning Fallacy** (ch. 91); **Authority Bias** (ch. 9); **Hindsight Bias** (ch. 14); **Overconfidence Effect** (ch. 15); **Illusion of Control** (ch. 17); **Hedonic Treadmill** (ch. 46); **Black Swan** (ch. 75)

41

THE DECEPTION OF SPECIFIC CASES

Conjunction Fallacy

Chris is 35. He studied social philosophy and has had an interest in developing countries since he was a teenager. After graduation, he worked for two years with the Red Cross in West Africa and then for three years in its Geneva headquarters, where he rose to head of the African aid department. He then completed an MBA, writing his thesis on corporate social responsibility. What is more likely? A) Chris works for a major bank or B) Chris works for a major bank, where he runs its Third World foundation. A or B?

Most people will opt for B. Unfortunately, it's the wrong answer. Option B does not only say that Chris works for a major bank, but also that an additional condition has been met. Employees who work specifically within a bank's Third World foundation comprise a tiny subset of bankers. Therefore, option A is much more likely. The *conjunction fallacy* is at play when such a subset seems larger than the entire set – which by definition cannot be the case. Nobel laureate Daniel Kahneman and Amos Tversky have studied this extensively.

We are easy prey for the *conjunction fallacy* because we have an innate attraction to 'harmonious' or 'plausible' stories. The more convincingly, impressively or vividly Chris the aid worker is portrayed, the greater the risk of false reasoning. If I had put it a different way, you would have recognised the extra details as overly specific: for example 'Chris is 35. What is more likely? A) Chris works for a bank or B) Chris works for a bank in New York, where his office is on the twenty-fourth floor, overlooking Central Park.'

Here's another example: What is more likely? A) 'Seattle airport is closed. Flights are cancelled.' B) 'Seattle airport is closed due to bad weather. Flights are cancelled.' A or B? This time, you have it: A is more likely since B implies that an additional condition has been met, namely bad weather. It could be that a bomb threat, accident or strike closed the airport; however, when faced with a 'plausible' story, we don't stop to consider such things. Now that you are aware of this, try it out with friends. You will see that most pick B.

Even experts are not immune to the *conjunction fallacy*. In 1982, at an international conference for future research, experts – all of them academics – were divided into two groups. To group A, Daniel Kahneman presented the following forecast for 1983: 'Oil consumption will decrease by 30%.' Group B heard that: 'A dramatic rise in oil prices will lead to a 30% reduction in oil consumption.' Both groups had to indicate how likely they considered the scenarios. The result was clear: group B felt much more strongly about its forecast than group A did.

Kahneman believes that two types of thinking exist. The first kind is intuitive, automatic and direct. The second is conscious, rational, slow, laborious and logical. Unfortunately, intuitive thinking draws conclusions long before the conscious mind does. For example, I experienced this after the 9/11 attacks on the World Trade Center. I wanted to take out travel insurance and came across a firm that offered special 'terrorism cover'. Although other policies protected against all possible incidents (including terrorism), I automatically fell for the offer. The high point of the whole farce was that I was willing to pay even more for this enticing yet redundant add-on.

In conclusion: forget about left brains and right brains. The difference between intuitive and conscious thinking is much more significant. With important decisions, remember that, at the intuitive level, we have a soft spot for plausible stories. Therefore, be on the lookout for convenient details and happy endings. Remember: if an additional condition has to be met, no matter how plausible it sounds, it will become less, not more, likely.

See also **Base-Rate Neglect** (ch. 28); **Story Bias** (ch. 13)

42

IT'S NOT WHAT YOU SAY, BUT HOW YOU SAY IT

Framing

> Consider these two statements:
> 'Hey, the trashcan is full!'
> 'It would be really great if you could empty the trash, honey.'

C'est le ton qui fait la musique: it's not what you say, but how you say it. If a message is communicated in different ways, it will also be received in different ways. In psychologists' jargon, this technique is called *framing*.

We react differently to identical situations, depending on how they are presented. Kahneman and Tversky conducted a survey in the 1980s in which they put forward two options for an epidemic-control strategy. The lives of 600 people were at stake, they told participants. 'Option A saves 200 lives.' 'Option B offers a 33% chance that all 600 people will survive, and a 66% chance that no one will survive.' Although options A and B were comparable (with 200 survivors expected), the majority of respondents chose A – remembering the adage: a bird in the hand is worth two in the bush. It became really interesting when the same options were *reframed*. 'Option A *kills* 400 people', 'Option B offers a 33% chance that no one will die, and a 66%

chance that all 600 will die.' This time, only a fraction of respondents chose A and the majority picked B. The researchers observed a complete U-turn from almost all involved. Depending on the phrasing – survive or die – the respondents made completely different decisions.

Another example: researchers presented a group of people with two kinds of meat, '99% fat free' and '1% fat', and asked them to choose which was healthier. Can you guess which they picked? Bingo: respondents ranked the first type of meat as healthier, even though both were identical. Next came the choice between '98% fat free' and '1% fat'. Again, most respondents chose the first option – despite its higher fat content.

Glossing is a popular type of *framing*. Under its rules, a tumbling share price becomes 'correction'. An overpaid acquisition price is branded 'goodwill'. In every management course, a problem magically transforms into an 'opportunity' or a 'challenge'. A person who is fired is 'reassessing his career'. A fallen soldier – regardless of how much bad luck or stupidity led to his death – turns into a 'war hero'. Genocide translates to 'ethnic cleansing'. A successful emergency landing, for example on the Hudson River, is celebrated as a 'triumph of aviation'. (Shouldn't a textbook landing on a runway count as an even bigger triumph of aviation?)

Have you ever looked more closely at the prospectus for financial products – for example, ETFs (exchange-traded funds)? Generally the brochure illustrates the product's performance in recent years, going back just far enough for the nicest possible upward curve to emerge. This is also *framing*. Another example is a simple piece of bread. Depending on how it is *framed*, as either the 'symbolic' or the 'true' body of Christ, it can split a religion, as happened in the sixteenth century with the Reformation.

Framing is used to good effect in commerce, too. Consider used cars. You are led to focus on just a few factors, whether the message is delivered through a sales- man, a sign touting certain features, or even your own criteria. For example, if the car has low mileage and good tyres, you home in on this and overlook the state of the engine, the brakes or the interior. Thus, the mileage and tyres become the main selling points and frame our deci- sion to buy. Such oversight is only natural, though, since it is difficult to take in all possible pros and cons. Interest- ingly, had other frames been used to tout the car we might have decided very differently.

Authors are conscious framers, too. A crime novel would be rather dull if, from page one, the murder were shown as it happened – stab by stab, as it were. Even though we even- tually discover the motives and murder weapons, the novelist's *framing* injects thrills and suspense into the story.

In conclusion: realise that whatever you communicate contains some element of *framing*, and that every fact – even if you hear it from a trusted friend or read it in a reputable newspaper – is subject to this effect, too. Even this chapter.

See also **Contrast Effect** (ch. 10); **Fear of Regret** (ch. 82); **Loss Aversion** (ch. 32); **Reciprocity** (ch. 6); **The Anchor** (ch. 30); **Sleeper Effect** (ch. 70)

43

WHY WATCHING AND WAITING IS TORTURE

Action Bias

In a penalty situation in soccer, the ball takes less than 0.3 seconds to travel from the player who kicks the ball to the goal. There is not enough time for the goalkeeper to watch the ball's trajectory. He must take a decision before the ball is kicked. Soccer players who take penalty kicks shoot one third of the time at the middle of the goal, one third of the time at the left and one third of the time at the right. Surely goalkeepers have spotted this, but what do they do? They dive either to the left or to the right. Rarely do they stay standing in the middle – even though roughly a third of all balls land there. Why on earth would they jeopardise saving these penalties? The simple answer: appearance. It looks more impressive and feels less embarrassing to dive to the wrong side than to freeze on the spot and watch the ball sail past. This is the *action bias*: look active, even if it achieves nothing.

This study comes from the Israeli researcher Michael Bar-Eli, who evaluated hundreds of penalty shoot-outs. But not just goalkeepers fall victim to the *action bias*. Suppose a group of youths exits a nightclub and begins to argue, shouting at each other and gesturing wildly. The situation is close to escalating into an all-out brawl. The police officers in the area – some young, some more senior – hold back, monitor the scene from a distance and intervene only when the first casualties appear. If no experienced officers are involved, this situation often ends differently: young, overzealous officers succumb to the *action bias* and dive in immediately. A study has revealed that later intervention, thanks to the calming presence of senior officers, results in fewer casualties.

The *action bias* is accentuated when a situation is new or unclear. When starting out, many investors act like the young, gung-ho police officers outside the nightclub: they can't yet judge the stock market so they compensate with a sort of hyperactivity. Of course this is a waste of time. As Charlie Munger sums up his approach to investing: 'We've got . . . discipline in avoiding just doing any damn thing just because you can't stand inactivity.'

The *action bias* exists even in the most educated circles. If a patient's illness cannot yet be diagnosed with certainty, and doctors must choose between intervening (i.e. prescribing something) or waiting and seeing, they are prone to taking action. Such decisions have nothing to do with profiteering, but rather with the human tendency to want to do anything but sit and wait in the face of uncertainty.

So what accounts for this tendency? In our old hunter-gatherer environment (which suited us quite well), action trumped reflection. Lightning-fast reactions were essential to survival; deliberation could be fatal. When our ancestors saw a silhouette appear at the edge of the forest – something that looked a lot like a sabre-tooth tiger – they did not take a pew to muse over what it might be. They hit the road – and fast. We are the descendants of these quick responders. Back then, it was better to run away once too often.

However, our world today is different; it rewards reflection, even though our instincts may suggest otherwise.

Although we now value contemplation more highly, outright inaction remains a cardinal sin. You get no honour, no medal, no statue with your name on it if you make exactly the right decision by *waiting* – for the good of the company, the state, even humanity. On the other hand, if you demonstrate decisiveness and quick judgement, and the situation improves (though perhaps coincidentally), it's quite possible your boss, or even the mayor, will shake your hand. Society at large still prefers rash action to a sensible wait-and-see strategy.

In conclusion: in new or shaky circumstances, we feel compelled to do something, anything. Afterward we feel better, even if we have made things worse by acting too quickly or too often. So, though it might not merit a parade in your honour, if a situation is unclear, hold back until you can assess your options. 'All of humanity's problems stem from man's inability to sit quietly in a room alone,' wrote Blaise Pascal. At home, in his study.

See also **Omission Bias** (ch. 44); **Overthinking** (ch. 90); **Procrastination** (ch. 85); **The It'll-Get-Worse-Before-It-Gets-Better Fallacy** (ch. 12); **Inability to Close Doors** (ch. 68)

44

WHY YOU ARE EITHER THE SOLUTION – OR THE PROBLEM

Omission Bias

You are on a glacier with two climbers. The first slips and falls into a crevasse. He might survive if you call for help, but you don't, and he perishes. The second climber you actively push into the ravine, and he dies shortly afterwards. Which weighs more heavily on your conscience?

Considering the options rationally, it's obvious that both are equally reprehensible, resulting as they do in death for your companions. And yet something makes us rate the first option, the passive option, as less horrible. This feeling is called the *omission bias*. It crops up where both action and inaction lead to cruel consequences. In such cases, we tend to prefer inaction; its results seem more anodyne.

Suppose you are the head of the Federal Drug Administration. You must decide whether or not to approve a drug for the terminally ill. The pills can have fatal side effects: they kill 20% of patients on the spot, but save the lives of the other 80% within a short period of time. What do you decide?

Most would withhold approval. To them, waving through a drug that takes out every fifth person is a worse act than failing to administer the cure to the other 80% of patients. It is an absurd decision, and a perfect example of the *omission bias*. Suppose that you are aware of the bias and decide to approve the drug in the name of reason and decency. Bravo. But what happens when the first patient dies? A media storm ensues, and soon you find yourself out of a job. As a civil servant or politician, you would do well to take the ubiquitous *omission bias* seriously – and even foster it.

Case law shows how ingrained such 'moral distortion' is in our society. Active euthanasia, even if it is the explicit wish of the dying, is punishable by law, whereas deliberate refusal of life-saving measures is legal (for example, following so-called DNR orders – do not resuscitate).

Such thinking also explains why parents feel it is perfectly acceptable not to vaccinate their children, even though vaccination discernibly reduces the risk of catching the disease. Of course, there is also a very small risk of getting sick from the vaccine. Overall, however, vaccination makes sense. Vaccination not only protects the children, but society too. A person who is immune to the disease will never infect others. Objectively, if non-vaccinated children ever contracted one of these sicknesses, we could accuse the parents of actively harming them. But this is exactly the point: Deliberate inaction somehow seems less grave than a comparable action – say, if the parents intentionally infected them.

The *omission bias* lies behind the following delusions: we wait until people shoot themselves in the foot rather than taking aim ourselves. Investors and business journalists are more lenient on companies that develop no new products than they are on those that produce bad ones, even though both roads lead to ruin. Sitting passively on a bunch of miserable shares feels better than actively buying bad ones. Building no emission filter into a coal plant feels superior to removing one for cost reasons. Failing to insulate your house is more acceptable than burning the spared fuel for your own amusement. Neglecting to declare income tax is less immoral than faking tax documents, even though the state loses out either way.

In the previous chapter, we met the *action bias*. Is it the opposite of the *omission bias*? Not quite. The action bias causes us to offset a lack of clarity with futile hyperactivity, and comes into play when a situation is fuzzy, muddy or contradictory The *omission bias*, on the other hand, usually abounds where the situation is intelligible: a future misfortune might be averted with direct action, but this insight doesn't motivate us as much as it should.

The *omission bias* is very difficult to detect – after all, action is more noticeable than inaction. In the 1960s student movements coined a punchy slogan to condemn it: 'If you're not part of the solution, you're part of the problem.'

See also **Volunteer's Folly** (ch. 65); **Action Bias** (ch. 43); **Procrastination** (ch. 85)

45

DON'T BLAME ME

Self-Serving Bias

Do you ever read annual reports, paying particular attention to the CEO's comments? No? That's a pity, because there you'll find countless examples of this next error, which we all fall for at one time or another. For example, if the company has enjoyed an excellent year, the CEO catalogues his indispensable contributions: his brilliant decisions, tireless efforts and cultivation of a dynamic corporate culture. However, if the company has had a miserable year, we read about all sorts of other dynamics: the unfortunate exchange rate, governmental interference, the malicious trade practices of the Chinese, various hidden tariffs, subdued consumer confidence and so on. In short: we attribute success to ourselves and failures to external factors. This is the *self-serving bias*.

Even if you have never heard the expression, you definitely know the *self-serving bias* from high school. If you got an A, you were solely responsible; the top grade reflected your intelligence, hard work and skill. And if you flunked? The test was clearly unfair.

But grades don't matter to you any more: perhaps the stock market has taken their place. There, if you make a profit, you applaud yourself. If your portfolio performs miserably, the blame lies exclusively with 'the market' (whatever you imply by this) – or maybe that useless investment adviser. I, too, have periods where I'm a power user of the *self-serving bias*: if my new novel rockets up the bestseller list, I clap myself on the shoulder. Surely this is my best book yet! But, if it disappears in the flood of new releases, it is because the readers simply don't recognise good literature when they see it. And if critics slay it, it is clearly a case of jealousy.

To investigate this bias, researchers put together a personality test and afterward, allocated the participants good or bad scores at random. Those who got scored highly found the test thorough and fair; low scorers rated it completely useless. So why do we attribute success to our own skill and ascribe failure to other factors? There are many theories. The simplest explanation is probably this: it feels good. Plus, it doesn't cause any major harm. If it did, evolution would have eliminated it over the past hundred thousand years. But beware: in a modern world with many hidden risks, the *self-serving bias* can quickly lead to catastrophe. Richard Fuld, the self-titled 'master of the universe', might well endorse this. He was the almighty CEO of the investment bank Lehman Brothers until it went bankrupt in 2008. It would not surprise me if he still called himself 'master of the universe', blaming government inaction for the bank's collapse.

In SAT tests, students can score between 200 and 800 points. When asked their results a year later, they tend to boost their scores by around 50 points. Interestingly, they are neither lying nor exaggerating; they are simply 'enhancing' the result a little – until they start to believe the new score themselves.

In the building where I live, five students share an apartment. I meet them now and again in the elevator, and I decided to ask them separately how often they take out the trash. One said he did it every second time. Another: every third time. Roommate #3, cursing because his garbage bag had split, reckoned he did it pretty much every time, say 90%. Although their answers should have added up to 100%, these boys achieved an impressive 320%! The five systematically overestimated their roles – and so, are no different to any of us. In married couples, the same thing happens: it's been shown that both men and women over-estimate their contribution to the health of the marriage. Each assumes their input is more than 50%.

So, how can we dodge the *self-serving bias*? Do you have friends who tell you the truth – no holds barred? If so, consider yourself lucky. If not, do you have at least one enemy? Good. Invite him or her over for coffee and ask for an honest opinion about your strengths and weaknesses. You will be forever grateful you did.

See also **Hindsight Bias** (ch. 14); **Overconfidence Effect** (ch. 15); **Not-Invented-Here Syndrome** (ch. 74); **Survivorship Bias** (ch. 1); **Beginner's Luck** (ch. 49); **Cognitive Dissonance** (ch. 50); **Forer Effect** (ch. 64); **Introspection Ilusion** (ch. 67); **Cherry-Picking** (ch. 96)

46

BE CAREFUL WHAT
YOU WISH FOR

Hedonic Treadmill

Suppose one day, the phone rings. An excited voice tells you that you have just scooped the lottery jackpot – $10 million! How would you feel? And, how long would you feel like that? Another scenario. The phone rings and you learn that your best friend has passed away. Again, how would you feel, and for how long?

In chapter 40, we examined the miserable accuracy of predictions, for example in the fields of politics, economics and social events. We concluded that self-appointed experts are of no more use than a random forecast generator. So, moving on to a new area: how well can we predict our feelings? Are we experts on ourselves? Would winning the lottery make us the happiest people alive for years to come? Harvard psychologist Dan Gilbert says no. He has studied lottery winners and discovered that the happiness effect fizzles out after a few months. So, a little while after you receive the big cheque, you will be as content or as discontent as you were before. He calls this 'affective forecasting'; our inability to correctly predict our own emotions.

A friend, a banking executive, whose enormous income was beginning to burn a hole in his pocket, decided to build

himself a new home away from the city. His dream materi-
alised into a villa with ten rooms, a swimming pool and an
enviable view of the lake and mountains. For the first few
weeks, he beamed with delight. But soon the cheerfulness
disappeared, and six months later he was unhappier than
ever. What happened? As we now know, the happiness
effect evaporates after a few months. The villa was no
longer his dream. 'I come home from work, open the door
and . . . nothing. I feel as indifferent about the villa as I did
about my one-room student apartment.' To make things
worse, the poor guy now faced a one-hour commute twice
a day. This may sound tolerable, but studies show that
commuting by car represents a major source of discontent
and stress, and people hardly ever get used to it. In other
words, whoever has no innate affinity for commuting will
suffer every day – twice a day. Anyhow, the moral of the
story is that the dream villa had an overall negative effect
on my friend's happiness.

Many others fare no better: People who change or
progress in their careers are, in terms of happiness, right
back where they started after around three months. The
same goes for people who buy the latest Porsche. Science
calls this effect the *hedonic treadmill*: we work hard,
advance and are able to afford more and nicer things, and
yet this doesn't make us any happier.

So how do negative events affect us – say, a spinal cord
injury or the loss of a friend? Here, we also overestimate
the duration and intensity of future emotions. For example,
when a relationship ends it feels like life will never be the
same. The afflicted are completely convinced that they will
never again experience joy, but after three or so months
they are back on the dating scene.

Wouldn't it be nice if we knew exactly how happy a new car, career or relationship would make us? Well, this is doable in part. Use these scientifically rubber-stamped pointers to make better, brighter decisions: 1) Avoid negative things that you cannot grow accustomed to, such as commuting, noise or chronic stress. 2) Expect only short-term happiness from material things, such as cars, houses, lottery winnings, bonuses and prizes. 3) Aim for as much free time and autonomy as possible, since long-lasting positive effects generally come from what you actively do. Follow your passions even if you must forfeit a portion of your income for them. Invest in friendships. For most people, professional status achieves long-lasting happiness, as long as they don't change peer groups at the same time. In other words, if you ascend to a CEO role and fraternise only with other executives, the effect fizzles out.

See also **Forecast Illusion** (ch. 40); **Neomania** (ch. 69); **Envy** (ch. 86)

47

DO NOT MARVEL AT
YOUR EXISTENCE

Self-Selection Bias

Travelling from Philadelphia up to New York, I got stuck in a traffic jam. 'Why is it always me?' I groaned. Glancing to the opposite side of the road, I saw carefree southbound drivers racing past with enviable speed. As I spent the next hour crawling forward at a snail's pace, and started to grow restless from braking and accelerating, I asked myself whether I really was especially unlucky. Do I always pick the worst lines at the bank, post office and grocery store? Or do I just *think* I do?

Suppose that, on this highway, a traffic jam develops 10% of the time. The probability that I will get stuck in a jam on a particular day is not greater than the probability that one will occur. However, the likelihood that I will get stuck at a certain point in my journey is greater than 10%. The reason: because I can only crawl forward when in a traffic jam, I spend a disproportionate amount of time in this state. In addition, if the traffic is zooming along, the prospect never crosses my mind. But the moment it arises and I am stuck, I notice it.

The same applies to the lines at bank counters or traffic lights. Let's say the route between point A and point B has ten traffic lights. On average, one out of the ten will always be red and the others green. However, you might spend more than 10% of your total travel time waiting at a red light. If this doesn't seem right, imagine that you are travelling at near the speed of light. In this case, you would spend 99.99% (not 10%) of your total journey time waiting and cursing in front of red traffic lights.

Whenever we complain about bad luck, we must be wary of the so-called *self-selection bias*. My male friends often gripe about there being too few women in their companies, and my female friends groan that theirs have too few men. This has nothing to do with bad luck: the grumblers form part of the sample. The probability is high that a man will work in a mostly male industry. Ditto for women. On a grander scale, if you live in a country with a large proportion of men or women (such as China or Russia, respectively), you are likely to form part of the bigger group and accordingly feel hard done by. In elections, it is most probable that you will choose the largest party. In voting, it is most likely that your vote corresponds with the winning majority.

The *self-selection bias* is pervasive. Marketers sometimes stumble into the trap in this way: to analyse how much customers value their newsletter, they send out a questionnaire. Unfortunately, this reaches only one group: current subscribers, who are clearly satisfied, have time to respond and have not cancelled their subscriptions. The others make up no part of the sample. Result: the poll is worthless.

Not too long ago, a rather maudlin friend remarked that it bordered on the miraculous that he – yes, he! – ever existed. A classic victim of the *self-selection bias*. Only someone who is alive can make such an observation.

Nonentities generally don't consider their non-existence for too long. And yet, precisely the same delusion forms the basis of at least a dozen philosophers' books, as they marvel year in, year out at the development of language. I'm quite sympathetic to their amazement, but it is simply not justified. If language did not exist, philosophers could not revere it at all – in fact, there would be no philosophers. The miracle of language is tangible only in the environment in which it exists.

Particularly amusing is this recent telephone survey: a company wanted to find out, on average, how many phones (landline and cell) each household owned. When the results were tallied, the firm was amazed that not a single household claimed to have no phone. What a masterpiece.

See also **Alternative Paths** (ch. 39); **Feature-Positive Effect** (ch. 95); **Swimmer's Body Illusion** (ch. 2)

48

WHY EXPERIENCE CAN DAMAGE OUR JUDGEMENT

Association Bias

Kevin has presented his division's results to the company's board on three occasions. Each time, things have gone perfectly. And, each time, he has worn his green polka-dot boxer shorts. It's official, he thinks: these are my lucky underpants.

The girl in the jewellery store was so stunning that Kevin couldn't help buying the $10,000 engagement ring she showed him. Ten thousand bucks was way over his budget (especially for a second marriage), but for some reason he associated the ring with her and imagined his future wife would be just as dazzling.

Each year, Kevin goes to the doctor for a check-up. Generally, he is told that, for a man of 44, he is still in pretty good shape. Only twice has he left the practice with worrying news. Once the problem was his appendix, which was promptly removed. The other time it was a swollen prostate, which, upon further inspection, turned out to be a simple inflammation rather than cancer. Of course, on both occasions, Kevin was beside himself with worry when leaving the clinic – and coincidentally, both days were extremely hot. Since then, he has always felt uncomfortable on very warm days. If the temperature starts to heat up around one of his check-ups, he cancels straight away.

Our brain is a connection machine. This is quite practical: if we eat an unknown fruit and feel sick afterward, we avoid it in future, labelling the plant poisonous or at least unpalatable. This is how knowledge comes to be. However, this method also creates false knowledge. Russian scientist Ivan Pavlov was the first to conduct research into this phenomenon. His original goal was to measure salivation in dogs. He used a bell to call the dogs to eat, but soon the ringing sound alone was enough to make the dogs salivate. The animals' brains linked two functionally unrelated things – the ringing of a bell and the production of saliva.

Pavlov's method works equally well with humans. Advertising creates a link between products and emotions. For this reason, you will never see Coke alongside a frowning face or a wrinkly body. Coke people are young, beautiful and oh so fun, and they appear in clusters not seen in the real world.

These false connections are the work of the *association bias*, which also influences the quality of our decisions. For example, we often condemn bearers of bad news, since we automatically associate them with the message's content (otherwise known as *shoot-the-messenger syndrome*). Sometimes, CEOs and investors (unconsciously) steer clear of these harbingers, meaning the only news that reaches the upper echelons is positive, thus creating a distorted view of the real situation. If you lead a group of people, and don't want to fall prey to false connections, direct your staff to tell you only the bad news – and fast. With this, you overcompensate for the *shoot-the-messenger syndrome* and, believe me, you will still hear enough positive news.

In the days before email and telemarketing, travelling salesmen went door to door peddling their wares. One day, a particular salesman, George Foster, stood at a front door. The house turned out to be vacant, and unbeknownst to him, a tiny leak had been filling it with gas for weeks. The bell was also damaged, so when he pressed it, it created a spark and the house exploded. Poor George ended up in hospital, but fortunately he was soon back on his feet. Unfortunately, his fear of ringing doorbells had become so strong that for many years he couldn't go back to his job. He knew how unlikely a repeat of the incident was, but for all he tried, he just couldn't manage to reverse the (false) emotional connection.

The take-home message from all this is phrased most aptly by Mark Twain: 'We should be careful to get out of an experience only the wisdom that is in it – and stop there; lest we be like the cat that sits down on a hot stove-lid. She will never sit down on a hot stove-lid again – and that is well; but also she will never sit down on a cold one anymore.'

See also **Contagion Bias** (ch. 54); **False Causality** (ch. 37); **Beginner's Luck** (ch. 49); **Availability Bias** (ch. 11); **Affect Heuristic** (ch. 66)

49

BE WARY WHEN THINGS GET OFF TO A GREAT START

Beginner's Luck

In the last chapter, we learned about the *association bias* – the tendency to see connections where none exist. For example, regardless of how many big presentations he has nailed while wearing them, Kevin's green polka-dot underpants are no guarantee of success.

We now come to a particularly tricky branch of the *association bias*: creating a (false) link with the *past*. Casino players know this well; they call it *beginner's luck*. People who are new to a game and lose in the first few rounds are usually clever enough to fold. But whoever strikes lucky tends to keep going. Convinced of their above-average skills, these amateurs increase the stakes – but they will soon get a sobering wake-up call when the probabilities 'normalise'.

Beginner's luck plays an important role in the economy. Say company A buys smaller companies B, C and D one after the other. The acquisitions prove a success, and the directors believe they have a real skill for acquisitions. Buoyed by this confidence, they now buy a much larger company, E. The integration is a disaster. The merger proves too difficult to handle, the estimated synergies impossible to realise. Objectively speaking, this was foreseeable because in the previous acquisitions everything fell perfectly into place as if guided by a magical hand, so *beginner's luck* blinded them.

The same goes for the stock exchange. Driven by initial success, many investors pumped their life savings into Internet stocks in the late 1990s. Some even took out loans to capitalise on the opportunity. However, these investors overlooked one tiny detail: their amazing profits at the time had nothing to do with their stock-picking abilities. The market was simply on an upward spiral. Even the most clueless investors won big. When the market finally turned downward, many were left facing mountains of dot-com debt.

We witnessed the same delusions during the recent U.S. housing boom. Dentists, lawyers, teachers and taxi drivers gave up their jobs to 'flip' houses – to buy them and resell them straight away at higher prices. The first fat profits justified their career changes, but of course these gains had nothing to do with any specific skills. The housing bubble allowed even the most inept amateur brokers to flourish. Many investors became deeply indebted as they flipped even more and even bigger mansions. When the bubble finally burst, many were left with only a string of unsellable properties to their names.

In fact, history has no shortage of *beginner's luck*: I doubt whether Napoleon or Hitler would have dared launch a campaign against the Russians without the previous victories in smaller battles to bolster them.

But how do you tell the difference between *beginner's luck* and the first signs of real talent? There is no clear rule, but these two tips may help: first, if you are much better than others over a long period of time, you can be fairly sure that talent plays a part. (Unfortunately, though, you can never be 100%.) Second, the more people competing, the greater the chances are that one of them will repeatedly strike lucky. Perhaps even you. If, among ten competitors, you establish yourself as a market leader over many years, you can clap yourself on the back. That's a sure indication of talent. But, if you are top dog among 10 million players (i.e. in the financial markets) in one particular year, you shouldn't start visualising a Buffettesque financial empire just yet; it's extremely likely that you have simply been very fortunate.

Watch and wait before you draw any conclusions. *Beginner's luck* can be devastating, so guard against misconceptions by treating your theories as a scientist would: try to disprove them. As soon as my first novel, *Thirty-five*, was ready to go, I sent it to a single publisher, where it was promptly accepted. For a moment I felt like a genius, a literary sensation. (The chance that this publisher will take on a manuscript is one in 15,000.) To test my theory, I then sent the manuscript to ten other big publishers. And I got ten rejection letters. My notion was thus disproven, bringing me swiftly back down to earth.

See also **Survivorship Bias** (ch. 1); **Self-Serving Bias** (ch. 45); **Association Bias** (ch. 48); **False Causality** (ch. 37); **Illusion of Skill** (ch. 94)

50

SWEET LITTLE LIES

Cognitive Dissonance

A fox crept up to a vine. He gazed longingly at the fat, purple, overripe grapes. He placed his front paws against the trunk of the vine, stretched his neck and tried to get at the fruit, but it was too high. Irritated, he tried his luck again. He launched himself upward, but his jaw snapped only at fresh air. A third time he leapt with all his might – so powerfully that he landed back down on the ground with a thud. Still not a single leaf had stirred. The fox turned up his nose: 'These aren't even ripe yet. Why would I want sour grapes?' Holding his head high, he strode back into the forest.

The Greek poet, Aesop, created this fable to illustrate one of the most common errors in reasoning. An inconsistency arose when the fox set out to do something and failed to accomplish it. He can resolve this conflict in one of three ways: A) by somehow getting at the grapes, B) by admitting that his skills are insufficient, or C) by retrospectively reinterpreting what happened. The last option is an example of *cognitive dissonance*, or rather, its resolution.

Suppose you buy a new car. However, you regret your choice soon afterward: the engine sounds like a jet taking off and you just can't get comfortable in the driver's seat. What do you do? Giving the car back would be an admission of error (you don't want that!), and anyway, the dealer probably wouldn't refund all the money. So you tell yourself that a loud engine and awkward seats are great safety features that will prevent you from falling asleep at the wheel. Not so stupid after all, you think, and you are suddenly proud of your sound, practical purchase.

Leon Festinger and Merrill Carlsmith of Stanford University once asked their students to carry out an hour of excruciatingly boring tasks. They then divided the subjects into two groups. Each student in group A received a dollar (it was 1959) and instructions to wax lyrical about the work to another student waiting outside – in other words, to lie. The same was asked of the students in group B, with one difference: they were given $20 for the task. Later, the students had to divulge how they had really found the monotonous work. Interestingly, those who received only a dollar rated it as significantly more enjoyable and interesting. Why? One measly dollar was not enough for them to lie outright; instead they convinced themselves that the work was not that bad. Just as Aesop's fox reinterpreted the situation, so did they. The students who received more didn't have to justify anything. They had lied and netted $20 for it – a fair deal. They experienced no *cognitive dissonance*.

Suppose you apply for a job and discover you have lost out to another candidate. Instead of admitting that the other person was better suited, you convince yourself that you didn't want the job in the first place; you simply wanted to test your 'market value' and see if you could get invited for interview.

I reacted very similarly some time ago when I had to choose between investing in two different stocks. My chosen stock lost much of its value shortly after the purchase, whereas shares in the other stock, the one I hadn't invested in, skyrocketed. I couldn't bring myself to admit my error. Quite the reverse, in fact: I distinctly remember trying to convince a friend that, though the stock was experiencing teething problems, it still had more potential overall. Only *cognitive dissonance* can explain this remarkably irrational reaction. The 'potential' would indeed have been even greater if I had postponed the decision to purchase the shares until today. It was that friend who told me the Aesop fable. 'You can play the clever fox all you want – but you'll never get the grapes that way.'

> *See also* **Endowment Effect** (ch. 23); **Self-Serving Bias** (ch. 45); **Confirmation Bias** (ch. 7–8); **'Because' Justification** (ch. 52); **Effort Justification** (ch. 60)

51

LIVE EACH DAY AS IF IT WERE YOUR LAST – BUT ONLY ON SUNDAYS

Hyperbolic Discounting

You know the saying: 'Live each day as if it were your last.' It features at least three times in every lifestyle magazine, and has a slot in every self-help manual's standard repertoire, too. For such a clever line, it makes you none the wiser. Just imagine what would happen if you followed it to the letter: you would no longer brush your teeth, wash your hair, clean the apartment, turn up for work, pay the bills . . . In no time, you would be broke, sick and perhaps even behind bars. And yet, its meaning is inherently noble. It expresses a deep longing, a desire for immediacy. We place huge value on immediacy – much more than is justifiable. 'Enjoy each day to the fullest and don't worry about tomorrow' is simply not a smart way to live.

Would you rather receive $1,000 in a year or $1,100 in a year and a month? Most people will opt for the larger sum in thirteen months – where else will you find a monthly interest rate of 10% (or 120% per annum!). A wise choice, since the interest will compensate you generously for any risks you face by waiting the extra few weeks.

Second question: would you prefer $1,000 today cash on the table or $1,100 in a month? If you think like most people, you'll take the $1,000 straight away. This is amazing. In both cases, if you hold out for just a month longer, you get $100 more. In the first case, it's simple enough. You figure: 'I've already waited twelve months; what's one more?' Not in the second case. The introduction of 'now' causes us to make inconsistent decisions. Science calls this phenomenon *hyperbolic discounting*. Put plainly, the closer a reward is, the higher our 'emotional interest rate' rises and the more we are willing to give up in exchange for it. The majority of economists have not yet grasped that we respond so subjectively and inconsistently to interest rates. Their models still depend on constant interest rates and are correspondingly questionable.

Hyperbolic discounting, the fact that immediacy magnetises us, is a remnant of our animal past. Animals will never turn down an instant reward in order to attain more in the future. You can train rats as much as you like; they're never going to give up a piece of cheese today to get two pieces tomorrow. But wait a minute: don't squirrels manage to gather food and save it for much later? Yes, but that's pure instinct and – verifiably – has nothing to do with impulse control or learning.

And what about children? In the 60s, Walter Mischel conducted a famous experiment on delayed gratification. You can find a wonderful video of this on YouTube by typing in 'marshmallow experiment'. In it, a group of four-year-olds were each given a marshmallow. They could either eat it straight away or wait a couple of minutes and receive a second. Amazingly, very few children could wait. Even more amazingly, Mischel found that the capacity for delayed gratification is a reliable indicator of future career success. Patience is indeed a virtue.

The older we get and the more self-control we build up, the more easily we can delay rewards. Instead of twelve months, we happily wait thirteen to take home an additional $100. However, if we are offered an instant reward, the incentive has to be very high for us to postpone the fulfilment. Case in point: the exorbitant interest rates banks charge on credit-card debt and other short-term personal loans, both of which exploit our must-have-now instincts.

In conclusion: though instantaneous reward is incredibly tempting, *hyperbolic discounting* is still a flaw. The more power we gain over our impulses, the better we can avoid this trap. The less power we have over our impulses – for example when we are under the influence of alcohol – the more susceptible we are. Viewed from the other side, if you sell consumer products, give customers the option of getting their hands on the items straight away. Some people will be willing to pay extra just so they don't have to wait. Amazon makes a bundle from this: a healthy chunk of the next-day delivery surcharge goes directly into its coffers. 'Live each day as if it were your last' is a good idea – once a week.

See also **Decision Fatigue** (ch. 53); **Simple Logic** (ch. 63); **Procrastination** (ch. 85)

52

ANY LAME EXCUSE

'Because' Justification

Traffic jam on the highway between Los Angeles and San Francisco: surface repairs. I spent thirty minutes slowly battling my way through until the chaos was a distant scene in my rear view mirror. Or so I thought. Half an hour later, I was again bumper to bumper: more maintenance work. Strangely enough, my level of frustration was much lower this time. Why? Reassuringly cheerful signs along the road announced: 'We're renovating the highway for you!'

The jam reminded me of an experiment conducted by the Harvard psychologist Ellen Langer in the 1970s. For this, she went into a library and waited at a photocopier until a line had formed. Then she approached the first in line and said: 'Excuse me, I have five pages. May I use the Xerox machine?' Her success rate was 60 per cent. She repeated the experiment, this time giving a reason: 'Excuse me. I have five pages. May I use the Xerox machine, because I'm in a rush?' In almost all cases (94 per cent), she was allowed to go ahead. This is understandable: if people are in a hurry, you often let them cut in to the front of the line. She tried yet another approach, this time saying: 'Excuse me. I have five pages. May I go before you, because I have to make some copies?' The result was amazing. Even though the pretext was (ahem) paper-thin – after all, everyone was standing in line to make copies – she was allowed to pass to the front of the line in almost all cases (93 per cent).

When you justify your behaviour, you encounter more tolerance and helpfulness. It seems to matter very little if your excuse is good or not. Using the simple validation 'because' is sufficient. A sign proclaiming: 'We're renovating the highway for you' is completely redundant. What else would a maintenance crew be up to on a highway? If you hadn't noticed before, you realise what is going on once you look out the window. And yet this knowledge reassures and calms you. After all, nothing is more frustrating than being kept in the dark.

Gate A57 at JFK airport, waiting to board. An announcement comes over the loudspeaker: 'Attention, passengers. Flight 1234 is delayed by three hours.' Wonderful. I walked to the desk to find out why. And came back no more enlightened. I was furious: how dare they leave us waiting in ignorance? Other airlines have the decency to announce: 'Flight 5678 is delayed by three hours due to operational reasons.' A throwaway reason if there ever was one, but enough to appease passengers.

It seems people are addicted to the word 'because' – so much so that we use it even when it's not necessary. If you are a leader, undoubtedly you have witnessed this. If you provide no rallying call, employee motivation dwindles. It simply doesn't make the grade to say that the purpose of your shoe company is to manufacture footwear. No: today, higher purposes and the story behind the story are all-important; for example: 'We want our shoes to revolutionise the market' (whatever that means). 'Better arch support for a better world!' (whatever that means). Zappo's claims that it is in the happiness business (whatever that means).

If the stock market rises or falls by half a per cent, you will never hear the true cause from stock market commentators – that it is white noise, the culmination of an infinite number of market movements. No: people want a palpable reason and the commentator is happy to select one. Whatever explanation he utters will be meaningless – with frequent blame applied to the pronouncements of Federal Reserve Bank presidents.

If someone asks why you have yet to complete a task, it's best to say: 'Because I haven't got around to it yet.' It's a pathetic excuse (had you done so, the conversation wouldn't be taking place), but it usually does the trick without the need to scramble for more plausible reasons.

One day I watched my wife carefully separating black laundry from blue. As far as I know, this effort isn't necessary. Both are dark colours, right? Such logic has managed to keep my clothes run-free for many years. 'Why do you do that?' I asked. 'Because I prefer to wash them separately.' For me, a perfectly fine answer.

Never leave home without 'because'. This unassuming little word greases the wheels of human interaction. Use it unrestrainedly.

See also **Cognitive Dissonance** (ch. 50); **Story Bias** (ch. 13); **Fallacy of the Single Cause** (ch. 97)

53

DECIDE BETTER – DECIDE LESS

Decision Fatigue

For weeks, you've been working to the point of exhaustion on this presentation. The PowerPoint slides are polished. Each figure in Excel is indisputable. The pitch is a paradigm of crystal-clear logic. Everything depends on your presentation. If you get the green light from the CEO, you're on your way to a corner office. If the presentation flops, you're on your way to the unemployment office. The CEO's assistant proposes the following times for the presentation: 8.00a.m., 11.30a.m. or 6.00p.m. Which slot do you choose?

The psychologist Roy Baumeister and his collaborator Jean Twenge once covered a table with hundreds of inexpensive items – from tennis balls and candles to T-shirts, chewing gum and Coke cans. He divided his students into two groups. The first group he labelled 'deciders', the second 'non-deciders'. He told the first group: 'I'm going to show you sets containing two random items and each time you have to decide which you prefer. At the end of the experiment I'll give you one item you can take home.' They were led to believe that their choices would influence which item they got to keep. To the second group, he said: 'Write down what you think about each item, and I'll pick one and give it to you at the end.' Immediately thereafter, he asked each student to put their hand in ice-cold water and hold it there for as long as possible. In psychology, this is a classic method to measure willpower or self-discipline; if you have little or none, you yank your hand back out of the water very quickly. The result: the deciders pulled their hands out of the icy water much sooner than the non-deciders did. The intensive decision-making had drained their willpower – an effect confirmed in many other experiments.

Making decisions is exhausting. Anyone who has ever configured a laptop online or researched a long trip – flight, hotels, activities, restaurants, weather – knows this well: after all the comparing, considering and choosing, you are exhausted. Science calls this *decision fatigue*.

Decision fatigue is perilous: as a consumer, you become more susceptible to advertising messages and impulse buys. As a decision-maker, you are more prone to erotic seduction. Willpower is like a battery. After a while it runs out and needs to be recharged. How do you do this? By taking a break, relaxing and eating something. Willpower plummets to zero if your blood sugar falls too low. IKEA knows this only too well. On the trek through its maze-like display areas and towering warehouse shelves, *decision fatigue* sets in. For this reason, its restaurants are located right in the middle of the stores. The company is willing to sacrifice some of its profit margin so that you can top up your blood sugar on Swedish treats before resuming your hunt for the perfect candlesticks.

Four prisoners in an Israeli jail petitioned the court for early release. Case 1 (scheduled for 8.50a.m.): an Arab sentenced to 30 months in prison for fraud. Case 2 (scheduled for 1.27p.m.): a Jew sentenced to 16 months for assault. Case 3 (scheduled for 3.10p.m.): a Jew sentenced to 16 months for assault. Case 4 (scheduled for 4.35p.m.): an Arab sentenced to 30 months for fraud. How did the judges decide? More significant than the detainees' allegiance or the severity of their crimes was the judges' *decision fatigue*. The judges granted requests 1 and 2 because their blood sugar was still high (from breakfast or lunch). However, they struck out applications 3 and 4 because they could not summon enough energy to risk the consequences of an early release. They took the easy option (the status quo) and the men remained in jail. A study of hundreds of verdicts shows that within a session, the percentage of 'courageous' judicial decisions gradually drops from 65% to almost zero, and after a recess, returns to 65%. So much for the careful deliberations of Lady Justice. But, as long as you have no upcoming trials, all is not lost: you now know when to present your project to the CEO.

See also **Paradox of Choice** (ch. 21); **Hyperbolic Discounting** (ch. 51); **Simple Logic** (ch. 63); **Default Effect** (ch. 81)

54

WOULD YOU WEAR
HITLER'S SWEATER?

Contagion Bias

Following the collapse of the Carolingian Empire in the ninth century, Europe, especially France, descended into anarchy. Counts, commanders, knights and other local rulers were perpetually embroiled in battles. The ruthless warriors looted farms, raped women, trampled fields, kidnapped pastors and set convents alight. Both the church and the unarmed farmers were powerless against the nobles' savage warmongering.

In the tenth century, a French bishop had an idea. He asked the princes and knights to assemble in a field. Meanwhile, priests, bishops and abbots gathered all the relics that they could muster from the area and displayed them there. It was a striking sight: bones, blood-soaked rags, bricks and tiles – anything that had ever come in contact with a saint. The bishop, at that time a person who commanded respect, then called upon the nobles, in the presence of the relics, to renounce unbridled violence and attacks against the unarmed. In order to add weight to his demand, he waved the bloody clothes and holy bones in front of them. The nobles must have had enormous reverence for such symbols: the bishop's unique appeal to their conscience spread throughout Europe, promoting the

'Peace and Truce of God'. 'One should never underestimate the fear of saints in the Middle Ages and of saints' relics,' says American historian Philip Daileader.

As an enlightened person, you can only laugh at this silly superstition. But wait: what if I put it to you this way? Would you put on a freshly laundered sweater that Hitler had once worn? Probably not, right? So, it seems that you haven't lost all respect for intangible forces, either. Essentially, this sweater has nothing to do with Hitler any more. There isn't a single molecule of Hitler's sweat on it. However, the prospect of putting it on still puts you off. It's more than just a matter of respect. Yes, we want to project a 'correct' image to our fellow humans and to ourselves, but the thought puts us off even when we are alone and when we convince ourselves that touching this sweater does not endorse Hitler in any way. This emotional reaction is difficult to override. Even those who consider themselves quite rational have a hard time completely banishing the belief in mysterious forces (me included).

Mysterious powers of this kind can't simply be switched off. Paul Rozin and his research colleagues at the University of Pennsylvania asked test subjects to bring in photos of loved ones. These were pinned to the centre of targets and the subjects had to shoot darts at them. Riddling a picture with darts does no harm to the person in it, but nevertheless the subjects' hesitation was palpable. They were much less accurate than a control group that had shot at regular targets beforehand. The test subjects behaved as if a mystic force prevented them from hitting the photos.

The *contagion bias* describes how we are incapable of ignoring the connection we feel to certain items – be they from long ago or only indirectly related (as with the photos). A friend was a long-time war correspondent for the French public television channel France 2. Just as passengers on a Caribbean cruise take home souvenirs from each island – a straw hat or a painted coconut – my friend also collected mementoes from her adventures. One of her last missions was to Baghdad in 2003. A few hours after American troops stormed Saddam Hussein's government palace, she crept into the private quarters. In the dining room, she spotted six gold-plated wine glasses and promptly commandeered them. When I attended one of her dinner parties in Paris recently, the gilded goblets had pride of place on the dining table. 'Are these from Lafayette?' one person asked. 'No, they are from Saddam Hussein,' she said candidly. A horrified guest spat his wine back into the glass and began to splutter uncontrollably. I had to contribute: 'You realise how many molecules you've already shared with Saddam, simply by breathing?' I asked. 'About a billion per breath.' His cough got even worse.

See also **Association Bias** (ch. 48); **Affect Heuristic** (ch. 66)

55

WHY THERE IS NO SUCH THING AS AN AVERAGE WAR

The Problem with Averages

Suppose you're on a bus with forty-nine other people. At the next stop, the heaviest person in America gets on. Question: by how much has the average weight of the passengers increased? Four per cent? Five? Something like that. Suppose the bus stops again, and on gets Bill Gates. This time we are not concerned about weight. Question: by how much has the average *wealth* risen? Four per cent? Five? Far from it!

Let's calculate the second example quickly. Suppose each of fifty randomly selected individuals has assets of $54,000. This is the statistical middle value, the median. Then Bill Gates is added to the mix, with his fortune of around $59 billion. The average wealth has just shot up to $1.15 billion, an increase of more than two million per cent. A single outlier has radically altered the picture, rendering the term 'average' completely meaningless.

'Don't cross a river if it is (*on average*) four feet deep,' warns Nassim Taleb, from whom I have the above examples. The river can be very shallow – mere inches – for long stretches, but it might transform into a raging torrent that is twenty feet deep in the middle, in which case you could easily drown. Dealing in averages is a risky undertaking because they often mask the underlying distribution – the way the values stack up.

Another example: the average amount of UV rays you are exposed to on a June day is not harmful to your health. But if you were to spend the entire summer in a darkened office, then fly to Barbados and lie in the sun without sunscreen for a week solid, you would have a problem – even though, on average over the summer, you were not getting more UV light than someone who was outside regularly.

All this is quite straightforward and maybe you were aware of it already. For example, you drink one glass of red wine at dinner every evening. That's not a health issue. Many doctors recommend it. But if you drink no alcohol the entire year and on Dec 31 you gulp 356 glasses, which is equivalent to sixty bottles, you will have a problem, although the *average* over the year is the same.

Here's the update: in a complex world, distribution is becoming more and more irregular. In other words, we will observe the Bill Gates phenomenon in ever more domains. How many visits does an average website get? The answer is: there are no average websites. A handful of sites (such as the *New York Times*, Facebook or Google) garner the majority of visits, and countless other pages draw comparatively few. In such cases, mathematicians speak of the so-called power law. Take cities. There is one city on this planet with a population of more than 30 million: Tokyo. There are 11 cities with a population of between 20 and 30 million. There are 15 cities with a population of between 10 and 20 million. There are 48 cities with between 5 and 10 million inhabitants. And thousands (!) between 1 and 5 million. That's a power law.

A few extremes dominate the distribution, and the concept of average is rendered worthless.

What is the average size of a company? What is the average population of a city? What is an average war (in terms of deaths or duration)? What is the average daily fluctuation in the Dow Jones? What is the average cost overrun of construction projects? How many copies does an average book sell? What is the average amount of damage a hurricane wreaks? What is a banker's average bonus? What is the average success of a marketing campaign? How many downloads does an average iPhone app get? How much money does an average actor earn? Of course you can calculate the answers, but it would be a waste of time. These seemingly routine scenarios are subject to the power law.

To use just the final example: a handful of actors take home more than $10 million per year, while thousands and thousands live on the breadline. Would you advise your son or daughter to get into acting since the average wage is pretty decent? Hopefully not – wrong reason.

In conclusion: if someone uses the word 'average', think twice. Try to work out the underlying distribution. If a single anomaly has almost no influence on the set, the concept is still worthwhile. However, when extreme cases dominate (such as the Bill Gates phenomenon), we should discount the term 'average'. We should all take stock from novelist William Gibson: 'The future is already here – it's just not very evenly distributed.'

See also **Base-Rate Neglect** (ch. 28); **Simple Logic** (ch. 63); **Regression to Mean** (ch. 19); **Neglect of Probability** (ch. 26); **Gambler's Fallacy** (ch. 29)

56

HOW BONUSES DESTROY MOTIVATION

Motivation Crowding

A few months ago, a friend from Connecticut decided to move to New York City. This man had a fabulous collection of antiques, such as exquisite old books and hand-blown Murano glasses from generations ago. I knew how attached he was to them, and how anxious he would be handing them over to a moving company, so the last time I visited, I offered to carry the most fragile items with me when I returned to the city. Two weeks later I got a thank-you letter. Enclosed was a fifty-dollar bill.

For years, Switzerland has been considering where to store its radioactive waste. The authorities considered a few different locations for the underground repository, including the village of Wolfenschiessen in the centre of the country. Economist Bruno Frey and his fellow researchers at the University of Zurich travelled there and recorded people's opinions at a community meeting. Surprisingly, 50.8% were in favour of the proposal. Their positive response can be attributed to several factors: national pride, common decency, social obligation, the prospect of new jobs and so on. The team carried out the survey a second time, but this time they mentioned a hypothetical reward of $5,000 for each townsperson, paid for by Swiss taxpayers, if they were to accept the proposal. What happened? Results plummeted: only 24.6% were willing to endorse the proposal.

Another example is children's daycare centres. Daycare workers face the same issue the world over: parents collecting their children after closing time. The staff have no choice but to wait. They can hardly put the last remaining children in taxis or leave them on the kerb. To discourage parental tardiness, many nurseries have introduced fees for lateness, but studies show that tardiness has actually increased. Of course, they could have instituted a draconian penalty of, say, $500 for each hour – as they could have offered $1 million to each citizen of the small Swiss village. But that's beside the point. The point is: small – surprisingly small – monetary incentives crowd out other types of incentives.

The three stories illustrate one thing: money does not always motivate. Indeed, in many cases, it does just the opposite. When my friend slipped me that fifty, he undermined my good deed – and also tainted our friendship. The offer of compensation for the nuclear repository was perceived as a bribe, and cheapened the community and patriotic spirit. The nursery's introduction of late fees transformed its relationship with parents from interpersonal to monetary, and essentially legitimised their lateness.

Science has a name for this phenomenon: *motivation crowding*. When people do something for well-meaning, non-monetary reasons – out of the goodness of their hearts, so to speak – payments throw a wrench into the works. Financial reward erodes any other motivations.

Suppose you run a non-profit organisation. Logically, the wages you pay are quite modest. Nevertheless, your employees are highly motivated because they believe they are making a difference. If you suddenly introduce a bonus system – let's say a small salary increase for every donation secured – *motivation crowding* will commence. Your team will begin to snub tasks that bring no extra reward. Creativity, company reputation, knowledge transfer – none of this will matter any more. Soon, all efforts will zoom in on attracting donations.

So who is safe from *motivation crowding*? This tip should help: do you know any private bankers, insurance agents or financial auditors who do their jobs out of passion or who believe in a higher mission? I don't. Financial incentives and performance bonuses work well in industries with generally uninspiring jobs – industries where employees aren't proud of the products or the companies and do the work simply because they get a pay cheque. On the other hand, if you create a start-up, you would be wise to enlist employee enthusiasm to promote the company's endeavour rather than try to entice employees with juicy bonuses, which you couldn't pay anyway.

One final tip for those of you who have children: experience shows that young people are not for sale. If you want your kids to do their homework, practise musical instruments, or even mow the lawn once in a while, do not reach for your wallet. Instead, give them a fixed amount of pocket money each week. Otherwise, they will exploit the system and soon refuse to go to bed without recompense.

See also **Incentive Super-response Tedency** (ch. 18);
Reciprocity (ch. 6); **Social Loafing** (ch. 33)

57

IF YOU HAVE NOTHING TO SAY, SAY NOTHING

Twaddle Tendency

When asked why a fifth of Americans were unable to locate their country on a world map, Miss Teen South Carolina, a high-school graduate, gave this answer in front of rolling cameras: 'I personally believe that U.S. Americans are unable to do so because some people out there in our nation don't have maps, and I believe that our education like such as South Africa and the Iraq everywhere like such as and I believe that they should our education over here in the U.S. should help the U.S., should help South Africa and should help the Iraq and the Asian countries, so we will be able to build up our future.' The video went viral.

Catastrophic, you agree, but you don't waste too much time listening to beauty queens. OK, how about the following sentence? 'There is certainly no necessity that this increasingly reflexive transmission of cultural traditions be associated with subject-centred reason and future-oriented historical consciousness. To the extent that we become aware of the intersubjective constitution of freedom, the possessive-individualist illusion of autonomy as self-ownership disintegrates.'

Ring any bells? Top German philosopher and sociologist Jürgen Habermas in *Between Facts and Norms*.

Both of these are manifestations of the same phenomenon, the *twaddle tendency*. Here, reams of words are used to disguise intellectual laziness, stupidity, or underdeveloped ideas. Sometimes it works, sometimes not. For the beauty queen, the smokescreen strategy failed spectacularly. For Habermas, it might be working. The more eloquent the haze of words, the more easily we fall for them. If used in conjunction with the *authority bias* it can be especially dangerous as we are willing to accept the words without questioning them.

I myself have fallen for the *twaddle tendency* on many occasions. When I was younger, French philosopher Jacques Derrida fascinated me. I devoured his books, but even after intense reflection I still couldn't understand much. Subsequently his writings took on a mysterious aura, and the whole experience drove me to write my dissertation on philosophy. In retrospect, both were tomes of useless chatter – Derrida and my dissertation. In my ignorance, I had turned myself into a walking, talking smoke machine.

The *twaddle tendency* is especially rife in sport. Breathless interviewers push equally breathless football players to break down the components of the game, when all they want to say is: 'We lost the game – it's really that simple.' But the presenter has to fill airtime somehow – and seemingly the best method is by jabbering away and by compelling the athletes and coaches to join in. Jabber disguises ignorance.

This phenomenon has also taken root in the academic spheres. The fewer results a branch of science publishes, the more babble is necessary. Particularly exposed are economists, which can be seen in their comments and economic forecasts. The same is true for commerce on a smaller scale:

the worse-off a company is, the greater the talk of the CEO. The extra chatter extends to not just a lot of talking, but to hyperactivity, also designed to mask the hardship. A laudable exception is the former CEO of General Electric, Jack Welch. He once said in an interview: 'You would not believe how difficult it is to be simple and clear. People are afraid that they may be seen as a simpleton. In reality, just the opposite is true.'

In conclusion: verbal expression is the mirror of the mind. Clear thoughts become clear statements, whereas ambiguous ideas transform into vacant ramblings. The trouble is that, in many cases, we lack very lucid thoughts. The world is complicated, and it takes a great deal of mental effort to understand even one facet of the whole. Until you experience such an epiphany, it's better to heed Mark Twain: 'If you have nothing to say, say nothing.' Simplicity is the zenith of a long, arduous journey, not the starting point.

See also **Authority Bias** (ch.9); **Domain Dependence** (ch. 76); **Chauffeur Knowledge** (ch. 16)

58

HOW TO INCREASE THE AVERAGE IQ OF TWO STATES

Will Rogers Phenomenon

Let's say you run a small private bank. The bank manages the money of wealthy and mostly retired individuals. Two money managers – A and B – report to you. Money Manager A manages the money of a few ultra-high-net-worth individuals. Money Manager B has rich, but not extravagantly rich, clients to deal with. The board asks you to increase the average pool of money of both A and B – within six months. If you succeed, you receive a handsome bonus. If not, they'll find someone else to do it. Where do you start?

It's quite simple, actually: you take a client with a sizeable but not a huge pool of money from A and give it to B instead. In one fell swoop, this brings up A's average managed wealth as well as B's without you having to find a single new client. The only remaining question is: how will you spend your bonus?

Suppose you switch careers, and are now in charge of three hedge funds that invest primarily in privately held companies. Fund A has sensational returns, fund B's are mediocre and fund C's are miserable. You want to prove yourself to the world, so what's your master plan? You know how it works now: you move a few of A's shares to B and C, picking exactly those investments that have been pulling down A's average returns, but which are still profitable enough to fortify B and C. In no time, all three funds look much healthier. And, because the transformation happened in-house, you don't incur a single fee. Of course, the combined value of the trio hasn't risen by a single cent, but people will still pat you on the back.

This effect is called *stage migration* or the *Will Rogers phenomenon*, after an American comedian from Oklahoma. He is said to have joked that Oklahomans who pack up and move to California raise both states' average IQ. Since we rarely recognise such scenarios, let's drill the *Will Rogers phenomenon* to anchor it in your memory.

One good example is an auto franchise: let's say you take charge of two small branches in the same town with a total of six salesmen: numbers 1, 2 and 3 in branch A, and numbers 4, 5 and 6 in branch B. On average, salesman number 1 sells one car per week, salesman number 2 sells two cars per week and so on up to top salesman number 6, who shifts six cars each week. With a little calculation, you know that branch A sells two cars per salesman, whereas branch B is far ahead with an average of five cars per salesman per week. You decide to transfer salesman number 4 to branch A. What happens? Its average sales increase to 2.5 units per person. And branch B? It now consists of only two salesmen, numbers 5 and 6. Its average sales increase to 5.5 per person. Such switcheroo strategies don't change anything overall, but they create an impressive illusion. For this reason, journalists, investors and board members should be on special alert when they hear of rising averages in countries, companies, departments, cost centres or product lines.

A particularly deceitful case of the *Will Rogers phenomenon* is found in medicine. Tumours are usually broken down into four stages: the smallest and most treatable ones are classified as stage one; the worst are rated stage four. Their progression gives us the term *stage migration*. The survival rate is highest for stage-one patients and lowest for stage-four patients. Now, every year new procedures are released on to the market and allow for more accurate diagnosis. These new screening techniques reveal minuscule tumours that no doctor had ever noticed before. The result: patients who were erroneously diagnosed as healthy before are now counted as stage-one patients. The addition of relatively healthy people into the stage-one group increases the group's average life expectancy. A great medical success? Unfortunately not: mere *stage migration*.

See also **Intention-to-Treat Error** (ch. 98); **The Law of Small Numbers** (ch. 61)

59

IF YOU HAVE AN ENEMY, GIVE HIM INFORMATION

Information Bias

In his short story 'Del rigor en la ciencia', which consists of just a single paragraph, Jorge Luis Borges describes a special country. In this country, the science of cartography is so sophisticated that only the most detailed of maps will do – that is, a map with a scale of 1:1, as large as the country itself. Its citizens soon realise that such a map does not provide any insight, since it merely duplicates what they already know. Borges' map is an extreme case of the *information bias*, the delusion that more information guarantees better decisions.

Searching for a hotel in Miami a little while ago, I drew up a shortlist of five good offers. Straight away, one jumped out at me, but I wanted to make sure I had found the best deal and decided to keep researching. I ploughed my way through dozens of customer reviews and blog posts and clicked through countless photos and videos. Two hours later, I could say for sure which the best hotel was: the one I had liked at the start. The mountain of additional information did not lead to a better decision. On the contrary, if time is money, then I might as well have taken up residence at the Four Seasons.

Jonathan Baron from the University of Pennsylvania

asked physicians the following question: a patient presents symptoms that indicate with a probability of 80% that he is suffering from disease A. If this is not the case, the patient has either disease X or Y. Each of these diseases is equally bad, and each treatment results in similar side effects. As a doctor, what treatment would you suggest? Logically, you would opt for disease A and recommend the relevant therapy. Now suppose there is a diagnostic test that flashes 'positive' when disease X is present, and 'negative' when disease Y is detected. However, if the patient really does have disease A, the test results will be positive in 50% of the cases, and negative in the other 50%. Would you recommend conducting the test? Most doctors said yes – even though the results would be irrelevant. Assuming that the test result is positive, the probability of disease A is still much greater than that of disease X. The additional information contributes nothing of value to the decision.

Doctors are not the only professionals with a penchant for surplus information. Managers and investors are almost addicted to it. How often are studies commissioned one after the other, even though the critical facts are readily available? Additional information not only wastes time and money, it can also put you at a disadvantage. Consider this question: which city has more inhabitants – San Diego or San Antonio? Gerd Gigerenzer of the Max Planck Institute in Germany put this question to students in the Universities of Chicago and Munich. Sixty-two per cent of Chicago students guessed right: San Diego has more. But, astonishingly, every single German student answered correctly. The reason: all of them had heard of San Diego, but not necessarily of San Antonio, so they opted for the more familiar city. For the Chicagoans, however, both cities were household names. They had more information and it misled them.

Or, consider the hundreds of thousands of economists – in the service of banks, think tanks, hedge funds and governments – and all the white papers they have published from 2005 to 2007, the vast library of research reports and mathematical models. The formidable reams of comments. The polished PowerPoint presentations. The terabytes of information on Bloomberg and Reuters news services. The bacchanal dance to worship the god of information. It was all hot air. The financial crisis touched down and upended global markets, rendering the countless forecasts and comments worthless.

Forget trying to amass all the data. Do your best to get by with the bare facts. It will help you make better decisions. Superfluous knowledge is worthless, whether you know it or not. Daniel J. Boorstin put it right: 'The greatest obstacle to discovery is not ignorance – it is the illusion of knowledge.' And next time you are confronted by a rival, consider killing him – not with kindness but with reams of data and analysis.

See also **Overthinking** (ch. 90); **News Illusion** (ch. 99); **Base-Rate Neglect** (ch. 28)

60

HURTS SO GOOD

Effort Justification

John, a soldier in the U.S. Army, has just completed his paratrooper course. He waits patiently in line to receive the coveted parachute pin. At last, his superior officer stands in front of him, lines the pin up against his chest and pounds it in so hard that it pierces John's flesh. Ever since, he opens his top shirt button at every opportunity to showcase the small scar. Decades later, he has thrown away all the memorabilia from his time in the army, except for the tiny pin, which hangs in a specially made frame on his living room wall.

Mark singlehandedly restored a rusty Harley-Davidson. Every weekend and holiday went into getting it up and running; all the while his marriage was approaching breakdown. It was a struggle, but finally Mark's prized possession was road-ready and gleamed in the sunshine. Two years later, Mark desperately needs money. He sells all his possessions – the TV, the car, even his house – but not the bike. Even when a prospect offers double the actual value, Mark does not sell it.

John and Mark are victims of *effort justification*. When you put a lot of energy into a task, you tend to overvalue the result. Because John had to endure physical pain for the parachute pin, it outshines all his other awards. And since Mark's Harley cost him so many hours – and also nearly his wife – he prizes the bike so highly that he will never sell it.

Effort justification is a special case of *cognitive dissonance*. To have a hole punched in your chest for a simple merit badge borders on the absurd. John's brain compensates for this imbalance by overvaluing the pin, hyping it up from something mundane to something semi-sacred. All of this happens unconsciously and is difficult to prevent.

Groups use *effort justification* to bind members to them – for example, through initiation rites. Gangs and fraternities initiate new members by forcing them to withstand nauseating or vicious tests. Research proves that the harder the 'entrance exam' is to pass, the greater the subsequent pride and the value they attach to their membership. MBA schools play with *effort justification* in this way: they work their students day and night without respite, often to the point of exhaustion. Regardless of how useful or idiotic the coursework, once the students have the MBAs in the bag, they'll deem the qualification essential for their careers simply because it demanded so much of them.

A mild form of *effort justification* is the so-called *IKEA effect*. Furniture that we assemble ourselves seems more valuable than any expensive designer piece. The same goes for hand-knitted socks. To throw away a hand-crafted pair, even if they are tatty and outdated, is hard to do. Managers who put weeks of hard work into a strategy proposal will be incapable of appraising it objectively. Designers, copywriters, product developers, or any other professionals who brood over their creations are similarly guilty of this.

In the 1950s, instant cake mixes were introduced to the market. A surefire hit, thought the manufacturers. Far from it: housewives took an instant dislike to them – because they made things too easy. The firms reacted and made the preparation slightly more difficult (beating in an egg yourself). The added effort raised the women's sense of achievement and, with it, their appreciation for convenience food.

Now that you know about *effort justification*, you can rate your projects more objectively. Try it out: whenever you have invested a lot of time and effort into something, stand back and examine the result – *only* the result. The novel you've been tinkering with for five years and that no publisher wants: perhaps it's not Nobel-worthy after all. The MBA you felt compelled to do: would you really recommend it? And the woman you've been chasing for years: is she really better than bachelorette number two, who would say yes straight away?

See also **Sunk Cost Fallacy** (ch. 5); **Cognitive Dissonance** (ch. 50)

61

WHY SMALL THINGS LOOM LARGE

The Law of Small Numbers

You sit on the corporate board of a retail company with 1,000 stores. Half of the stores are in cities, the other half in rural areas. At the behest of the CEO, a consultant conducted a study on shoplifting and is now presenting his findings. Projected on to the wall in front are the names of the 100 branches that have the highest theft rates compared to sales. In bold letters above them is his eye-opening conclusion: 'The branches with the highest theft rate are primarily in rural areas.' After a moment of silence and disbelief, the CEO is first to speak: 'Ladies and gentlemen, the next steps are clear. From now on, we will install additional safety systems in all rural branches. Let's see those hillbillies steal from us then! Do we all agree?'

Hmmm, not completely. You ask the consultant to call up the 100 branches with the lowest theft rates. After some swift sorting, the list appears. Surprise, surprise: the shops with the lowest amount of shoplifting in relation to sales are also in rural areas! 'The location isn't the deciding factor,' you begin, smiling somewhat smugly as you gaze around the table at your colleagues. 'What counts is the size of the store. In the countryside, the branches tend to be small, meaning a single incident has a much larger influence on the theft rate. Therefore, the rural branches' rates vary greatly – much more than the larger city branches. Ladies and gentlemen, I introduce you to the *law of small numbers*. It has just caught you out.'

The *law of small numbers* is not something we understand intuitively. Thus people – especially journalists, managers and board members – continually fall for it. Let's examine an extreme example. Instead of the theft rate, consider the average weight of employees in a branch. Instead of 1,000 stores, we'll take just two: a mega-branch and a mini-branch. The big store has 1,000 employees; the small store just two. The average weight in the large branch corresponds roughly to the average weight of the population, say 170 pounds. Regardless of who is hired or fired, it will not change much. Unlike the small store: in these cases, the store manager's colleague, if rotund or reedy, will affect the average weight tremendously.

Let's go back to the shoplifting problem. We now understand why the smaller a branch is, the more its theft rate will vary – from extremely high to extremely low. No matter how the consultant arranges his spreadsheet, if you list all the theft rates in order of size, small stores will appear at the bottom, large stores will take up the middle – and the top slots? Small stores again. So, the CEO's conclusion was useless, but at least he doesn't need to go overboard on a security system for the small stores.

Suppose you read the following story in the newspaper: 'Start-ups employ smarter people. A study commissioned by the National Institute of Unnecessary Research has calculated the average IQ in American companies. The result: Start-ups hire MENSA material.' What is your first reaction? Hopefully a raised eyebrow. This is a perfect example of the *law of small numbers*. Start-ups tend to employ fewer people; therefore the average IQs will fluctuate much more than those of large corporations, giving small (and new) businesses the highest and lowest scores. The National Institute's study has zero significance. It simply confirms the laws of chance.

So, watch out when you hear remarkable statistics about any small entities: businesses, households, cities, data centres, anthills, parishes, schools etc. What is being peddled as an astounding finding is, in fact, a humdrum consequence of random distribution. In his latest book, Nobel Prize winner Daniel Kahneman reveals that even experienced scientists succumb to the *law of small numbers*. How reassuring.

See also **Exponential Growth** (ch. 34); **Will Rogers Phenomenon** (ch. 58)

62

HANDLE WITH CARE

Expectations

On 31 January 2006, Google announced its financial results for the final quarter of 2005. Revenue: up 97%. Net profit: up 82%. A record-breaking quarter. How did the stock market react to these phenomenal figures? In a matter of seconds, shares tumbled 16%. Trading had to be interrupted. When it resumed, the stock plunged another 15%. Absolute panic. One particularly desperate trader inquired on his blog: 'What's the best skyscraper to throw myself off?'

What had gone wrong? Wall Street analysts had anticipated even better results, and when those failed to materialise, $20 billion was slashed from the value of the media giant.

Every investor knows it's impossible to forecast financial results accurately. The logical response to a poor prediction would be: 'A bad guess, my mistake.' But investors don't react that way. In January 2006, when Juniper Networks announced eagerly anticipated earnings per share that were a *tenth* of a cent lower than analysts' forecasts, the share price fell 21% and the company's value plunged $2.5 billion. When expectations are fuelled in the run-up to an announcement, any disparity gives rise to draconian punishment, regardless of how paltry the gap is.

Many companies bend over backwards to meet analysts' predictions. To escape this terror, some began publishing their own estimates, so-called 'earnings guidance'. Not a smart move. Now, the market heeds only these internal forecasts – and studies them much more closely to boot. CFOs are forced to achieve these targets to the cent, and so must draw on all the accounting artifices available.

Fortunately, expectations can also lead to commendable incentives. In 1965, the American psychologist Robert Rosenthal conducted a noteworthy experiment in various schools. Teachers were told of a (fake) new test that could identify students who were on the verge of an intellectual spurt – so-called 'bloomers'. Twenty per cent of students were randomly selected and classified as such. Teachers remained under the impression that these were indeed high-potential students. After a year, Rosenthal discovered that these students had developed much higher IQs than other children in a control group. This effect became known as the *Rosenthal effect* (or *Pygmalion effect*).

Unlike the CEOs and CFOs who consciously tailor their performance to meet expectations, the teachers' actions were subconscious. Unknowingly, they probably devoted more time to the bloomers, and consequently, the group learned more. The prospect of brilliant students influenced the teachers so much that they ascribed not just better grades but also improved personality traits to the 'gifted' students – a tribute to the *halo effect*.

But how do we react to personal expectations? This brings us to the *placebo effect* – pills and therapies that are unlikely to improve health, but do so anyway. The *placebo effect* has been registered in one-third of all patients. But how it works is not well understood. All we know is that expectations alter the biochemistry of the brain and thus the whole body. Accordingly Alzheimer's patients cannot benefit from it: their condition impairs the area of the brain that deals with expectations.

Expectations are intangible, but their effect is quite real. They have the power to change reality. Can we deprogramme them? Is it possible to live a life free from expectations? Unfortunately not. But you can deal with them more cautiously. Raise expectations for yourself and for the people you love. This increases motivation. At the same time, lower expectations for things you cannot control – for example, the stock market. As paradoxical as it sounds, the best way to shield yourself from nasty surprises is to anticipate them.

See also **Black Swan** (ch. 75); **Forecast Illusion** (ch. 40); **Halo Effect** (ch. 38)

63

SPEED TRAPS AHEAD!

Simple Logic

Three easy questions. Grab a pen quickly and jot down your answers in the margin. First question: in a department store, a ping-pong paddle and a plastic ball cost $1.10. If the paddle costs $1 more, how much is the ball? Second question: in a textile factory, five machines take exactly five minutes to make five shirts. How many minutes will it take 100 machines to produce 100 shirts? And, the third question: a pond has water lilies growing in it. The flowers multiply quickly, each day doubling the area they take up. If it takes 48 days for the pond to be completely covered with water lilies, how many days will it take for it to be half covered? Don't read on until you have written down the answers.

For each of these questions, there is an intuitive answer – and a right one. The quick, intuitive answers come to mind first: 10 cents, 100 minutes and 24 days. But these are all wrong. The solutions are: five cents, five minutes and 47 days. How many did you answer correctly?

Thousands of people have taken this 'Cognitive Reflection Test' (CRT), which was developed by professor Shane Frederick. So far, students at the Massachusetts Institute of Technology (MIT) in Boston have fared best. On average, they got 2.18 correct answers. Students at Princeton

University came in second with an average of 1.63. Far below were students of the University of Michigan, who scored an average of 0.83. However, despite these neat rankings, averages in this case are not interesting. More interesting is how those who scored highly differ from the rest.

Here's a hint: would you prefer a bird in the hand or two in the bush? Frederick discovered that people with low CRT results tend to prefer a bird in the hand. They play it safe. After all, *something* is better than nothing. Those who score at least 2 or higher usually opt for the riskier option. They prefer the gamble. This is especially true for men.

One factor that separates the groups is their ability to control their impulses. In the chapter on *hyperbolic discounting*, we covered the seductive power of 'now'. Frederick put the following question to the participants: 'Would you rather have $3,400 now or $3,800 in a month?' In general, people with low CRT scores favour getting the smaller amount sooner. For them, waiting poses a challenge because they are more impulsive. This also applies to purchasing decisions. In contrast, people with high CRT results usually decide to wait the extra few weeks. They muster the willpower to turn down instant gratification – and are rewarded for it later on.

Thinking is more exhausting than sensing: rational consideration requires more willpower than simply giving in to intuition. In other words, intuitive people tend to scrutinise less. This led Harvard psychologist Amitai Shenhav and his research colleagues to investigate whether people's CRT results correlate with their faith. Americans with a high CRT score (the study was conducted only in the U.S.) are often atheists, and their convictions have been reinforced over the years. Participants with low CRT results, however, tend to believe in God and 'the immortality of the soul', and have often had divine experiences. This makes sense: the more intuitively people make decisions, the less rationally they query religious beliefs.

If you are less than pleased with your CRT score and want to improve it, start by greeting even the simplest logical questions with incredulity. Not everything that seems plausible is true. Reject the easy answers that pop into your head. So, one more try: you are travelling from A to B. On the way there, you drive at 100 mph and on the way back, at 50 mph. What was your average speed? 75? Slow down, slow down!

See also **Hyperbolic Discounting** (ch. 51); **Decision Fatigue** (ch. 53); **Exponential Growth** (ch. 34); **Gambler's Fallacy** (ch. 29); **The Problem With Averages** (ch. 55)

64

HOW TO EXPOSE A CHARLATAN

Forer Effect

Dear reader, it may surprise you, but I know you personally. This is how I would sum you up: 'You have a great need for other people to like and admire you. You have a tendency to be critical of yourself. You have a great deal of unused capacity, which you have not turned to your advantage. While you have some personality weaknesses, you are generally able to compensate for them. Your sexual adjustment has presented problems for you. Disciplined and self-controlled outside, you tend to be worrisome and insecure inside. At times you have serious doubts as to whether you have made the right decision or done the right thing. You prefer a certain amount of change and variety and become dissatisfied when hemmed in by restrictions and limitations. You pride yourself as an independent thinker and do not accept others' statements without satisfactory proof. You have found it unwise to be too frank in revealing yourself to others. At times you are extroverted, affable and sociable while at other times you are introverted, wary and reserved. Some of your aspirations tend to be pretty unrealistic. Security is one of your major goals in life.'

Do you recognise yourself? On a scale from 1 (poor) to 5 (excellent), how was my assessment?

In 1948, psychologist Bertram Forer crafted this exact passage using astrology columns from various magazines. He then gave it to his students to read, suggesting that each person was getting a personalised assessment. On average, the students rated their characterisations 4.3 out of five, i.e. they gave Forer an accuracy score of 86%. The experiment was repeated hundreds of times in the decades that followed, with virtually identical results.

Most likely you gave the text a 4 or 5, too. People tend to identify many of their own traits in such universal descriptions. Science labels this tendency the *Forer effect* (or the *Barnum effect*). The *Forer effect* explains why the pseudo-sciences work so well – astrology, astrotherapy, the study of handwriting, biorhythm analysis, palmistry, tarot-card readings and séances with the dead.

What's behind the *Forer effect*? First, the majority of statements in Forer's passage are so general that they relate to everyone: 'Sometimes you seriously doubt your actions.' Who doesn't? Second, we tend to accept flattering statements that don't apply to us: 'You are proud of your independent thinking.' Obviously! Who sees himself or herself as a mindless follower? Third, the so-called *feature positive effect* plays a part: the text contains no negative statements; it states only what we are, even though the absence of characteristics is an equally important part of a person's make-up. Fourth, the father of all the fallacies, the *confirmation bias*: we accept whatever corresponds to our self-image and unconsciously filter everything else out. What remains is a coherent portrait.

Whatever tricks astrologers and palm readers can turn, consultants and analysts can too: 'The stock has significant growth potential, even in a very competitive environment.

The company lacks the necessary impetus to fully realise and implement ideas from the development team. Management is made up of experienced industry professionals; however, hints of bureaucratisation are noticeable. A look at the profit and loss statement clearly shows that savings can be made. We advise the company to focus even more closely on emerging economies to secure future market share.' Sounds about right, no?

How do you rate the quality of such a guru – for example, an astrologer? Pick twenty people and secretly assign each a number. Have him characterise the people and write his assessments down on cards. To ensure anonymity, participants never find out their numbers. Afterward, each receives a copy of all the cards. Only when the majority of people identify 'their' description is there real talent at hand. I am still waiting.

See also **Feature-Positive Effect** (ch. 95); **Confirmation Bias** (chs. 7–8); **Self-Serving Bias** (ch. 45)

65

VOLUNTEER WORK IS FOR THE BIRDS

Volunteer's Folly

Jack, a photographer, is on the go from Monday to Friday. Commissioned by fashion magazines, he divides his time between Milan, Paris and New York and is constantly in search of the most beautiful girls, the most original designs and the perfect light. He is well known on the social circuit, and the money is great: $500 an hour, easy. 'That's as much as a commercial lawyer,' he brags to his buddies, 'and what I have in front of my lens looks a lot better than any banker.'

Jack leads an enviable life, but lately he has become more philosophical. It feels as if something has come between him and the fashion world. The selfishness of the industry suddenly repels him. Sometimes he lies in bed, staring at the ceiling, and yearns for more meaningful work. He would like to be selfless once again, to contribute something to the world, no matter how small.

One day his phone rings. It's Patrick, his former class-mate and current president of the local bird club: 'Next Saturday we're having our annual birdhouse drive. We're looking for volunteers to help us build birdhouses for endangered species. Afterwards we'll put them up in the woods. Do you have time? We're meeting at 8 o'clock in the morning. We should be done shortly after noon.'

What should Jack say if he really is serious about creating a better world? That's right, he should turn down the request. Why? Jack earns $500 an hour. A carpenter, $50. It would be much more sensible to work an extra hour as a photographer and then hire a professional carpenter for six hours to make good quality birdhouses (which Jack could never hope to accomplish). Taxes aside, he could donate the difference ($200) to the bird club. Doing so, his contribution would go much farther than if he grabbed a saw and rolled up his sleeves.

Nevertheless, it is highly likely that Jack will turn up bright and early next Saturday to build birdhouses. Economists call this *volunteer's folly*. It is a popular phenomenon: more than one-fourth of Americans volunteer their time. But what makes it folly? Among other things, if Jack chooses to cobble together a few birdhouses himself, it takes away work from a tradesman. Working a little longer and donating a portion of the earnings is the most effective contribution Jack can make. Hands-on volunteer work would be helpful only if he could make use of his expertise. If the bird club were planning a fundraising mail campaign and needed a professional photo, Jack could either shoot it himself or work an hour longer to hire another top photographer and donate the remainder.

So now we come to the thorny topic of altruism. Does selflessness exist at all or is it merely a balm to our egos? Although a desire to help the community motivates many volunteers, personal benefits such as gaining skills, experience, and contacts also play a big part. Suddenly we're not acting quite so selflessly. Indeed, many volunteers engage in what might be deemed 'personal happiness management', the benefits of which are sometimes far removed from the real cause. Strictly speaking, anyone who profits or feels even the slightest satisfaction from volunteering is not a pure altruist.

So does it mean Jack is a fool if he turns up, hammer in hand, on Saturday morning? Not necessarily. There is one group exempt from *volunteer's folly*: celebrities. If Bono, Kate Winslet or Mark Zuckerberg pose for photos while making birdhouses, cleaning oil-stained beaches or digging for earthquake victims, they lend something priceless to the situation: publicity. Therefore, Jack must critically assess whether he is famous enough to make his participation worthwhile. The same applies to you and me: if people don't double-take when they pass you on the street, the best way to contribute is with greenbacks rather than greenhorn labor.

See also **Déformation Professionnelle** (ch. 92); **Omission Bias** (ch. 44)

66

WHY YOU ARE A SLAVE
TO YOUR EMOTIONS

Affect Heuristic

What do you think of genetically modified wheat? It's a complex issue. You don't want to answer too hastily. A rational approach would be to consider the controversial technology's pros and cons separately. Write down the possible benefits, weight them in terms of importance, and then multiply them by the probability that they will occur. Doing so, you get a list of expected values. Next, do the same with the cons. List all the disadvantages, estimate their potential damage and multiply them by the likelihood of them happening. The positive sum minus the negative sum equals the net expected value. If it is above zero, you are in favour of genetically modified wheat. If the sum is below zero, you are against it. More than likely you have already heard of this approach. It is called 'expected value', and it features in most literature on decision theory. But just as probable is that you've never bothered to carry out such an evaluation. And without a doubt, none of the professors who wrote the textbooks turned to this method to select their spouses.

Truth be told, no one uses this method to make decisions. First of all, we lack enough imagination to list all the possible pros and cons. We are limited by what springs to mind; we can only conjure up what we have seen in our modest experience. It is hard to imagine a storm of the century if you're only 30 years old. Second, calculating small probabilities is impossible because we do not have enough data on rare events. The smaller the probability, the fewer data points we have and the higher the error rate on the exact probability – a vicious effect. Third, our brain is not built for such calculations. They require time and effort – not our preferred state. In our evolutionary past, whoever thought too long and hard vanished inside a predator's jaws. We are the descendants of quick decision-makers, and we rely on mental shortcuts called heuristics.

One of the most popular is the *affect heuristic*. An affect is a momentary judgement: something you like or dislike. The word 'gunfire' triggers a negative effect. The word 'luxury' produces a positive one. This automatic, one-dimensional impulse prevents you from considering risks and benefits to be independent variables, which indeed they are. Instead, the *affect heuristic* puts risks and benefits on the same sensory thread.

Your emotional reactions to issues such as nuclear power, organic vegetables, private schools or motorbikes determine how you assess their risks and benefits. If you like something, you believe that the risks are smaller and the benefits greater than they actually are. If you don't like something, the opposite is true. Risks and benefits appear to be dependent. Of course, in reality, they are not.

Even more impressive, suppose you own a Harley-Davidson. If you come across a study that states that driving one is riskier than previously thought, you will subconsciously tweak how you rate the benefits, deeming the experience 'an even greater sense of freedom'.

But how does an affect – the initial, spontaneous emotion – come to be? Researchers at the University of Michigan flashed either of three images for less than one hundredth of a second in front of participants: a smiling face, an angry face or a neutral figure. The subjects then had to indicate whether they liked a randomly selected Chinese character or not (the participants didn't speak Chinese). Most preferred symbols that immediately followed the smiling face. Seemingly insignificant factors influence our emotions. Here is another example where an insignificant factor plays a role. Researchers Hirschleifer and Shumway tested the relationship between the amount of morning sun and daily market performance in 26 major stock exchanges between 1982 and 1997. They found a correlation that reads much like a farmer's adage: if the sun is shining in the morning, the stock market will rise during the day. Not always, but often. Who would have thought that sunshine could move billions? The morning sun obviously has the same effect as a smiley face.

Whether we like it or not, we are puppets of our emotions. We make complex decisions by consulting our feelings, not our thoughts. Against our best intentions, we substitute the question, 'What do I think about this?' with 'How do I feel about this?' So, smile! Your future depends on it.

See also **Association Bias** (ch. 48); **Loss Aversion** (ch. 32); **Salience Effect** (ch. 83); **Contagion Bias** (ch. 54)

67

BE YOUR OWN HERETIC

Introspection Illusion

Bruce is in the vitamin business. His father founded the company when supplements were not yet a lifestyle product; a doctor had to prescribe them. When Bruce took over the operation in the early 1990s, demand skyrocketed. Bruce seized the opportunity with both hands and took out huge loans to expand production. Today, he is one of the most successful people in the business and president of a national association of vitamin manufactures. Since childhood, hardly a day has passed without him swallowing at least three multivitamins. A journalist once asked him if they do anything. He replied: 'I'm sure of it.' Do you believe him?

I have another question for you. Take any idea you are 100% sure of, perhaps that gold will rise over the next five years. Perhaps that God exists. Perhaps that your dentist is overcharging you. Whatever the belief, write it down in one sentence. Do you believe yourself?

I bet you consider your conviction more valid than Bruce's, right? Here's why: yours is an internal observation, whereas Bruce's is external. Crudely put, you can peek into your own soul, but not into his.

In Bruce's case, you might think: 'Come on, it's obviously in his interest to believe that vitamins are beneficial. After all, his wealth and social status depend on the success

THE ART OF THINKING CLEARLY

of the company. He has to maintain a family tradition. All his life he has gulped down pills, so he'll never admit that it was a waste of time.' For you, however, it's a different story: you have searched deep inside. You are completely impartial.

But how pure and honest is internal reflection? The Swedish psychologist Petter Johannson allowed test subjects to glimpse two portrait photos of random people and choose which face was more attractive. Then he showed them the preferred photo up close and asked them to describe the most attractive features. However, with a sleight of hand, he switched the pictures. Most participants failed to notice and proceeded to justify, in detail, why they favoured the image. The results of the study: introspection is not reliable. When we soul-search, we contrive the findings.

The belief that reflection leads to truth or accuracy is called the *introspection illusion*. This is more than sophistry. Because we are so confident of our beliefs, we experience three reactions when someone fails to share our views. Response 1: Assumption of ignorance. The other party clearly lacks the necessary information. If he knew what you know, he would be of the same opinion. Political activists think this way: they believe they can win others over through enlightenment. Reaction 2: Assumption of idiocy. The other person has the necessary information, but his mind is underdeveloped. He cannot draw the obvious conclusions. In other words, he's a moron. This reaction is particularly popular with bureaucrats who want to protect 'stupid' consumers from themselves. Response 3: Assumption of malice. Your counterpart has the necessary information – he even understands the debate – but he is deliberately confrontational. He has evil intentions. This is how many religious leaders and followers treat disbelievers: if they don't agree, they must be servants of the devil!

In conclusion: nothing is more convincing than your own beliefs. We believe that introspection unearths genuine self-knowledge. Unfortunately, introspection is, in large part, fabrication posing two dangers: first, the *introspection illusion* creates inaccurate predictions of future mental states. Trust your internal observations too much and too long, and you might be in for a very rude awakening. Second, we believe that our introspections are more reliable than those of others, which creates an illusion of superiority. Remedy: be all the more critical with yourself. Regard your internal observations with the same scepticism as claims from some random person. Become your own toughest critic.

See also **Illusion of Control** (ch. 17); **Self-Serving Bias** (ch. 45); **Confirmation Bias** (ch. 7–8); **Not-Invented-Here Syndrome** (ch. 74)

68

WHY YOU SHOULD SET FIRE TO YOUR SHIPS

Inability to Close Doors

Next to my bed, two dozen books are stacked high. I have dipped in and out of all of them, but am unable to part with even one. I know that sporadic reading won't help me achieve any real insights, despite the many hours I put in, and that I should really devote myself to one book at a time. So why am I still juggling all twenty-four?

I know a man who is dating three women. He is in love with all three and can imagine starting a family with any of them. However, he simply doesn't have the heart to choose just one, because then he would be passing up on the other two for good. If he refrains from deciding, all options remain open. The downside is that no real relationship will develop.

In the third century B.C., General Xiang Yu sent his army across the Yangtze River to take on the Qin Dynasty. While his troops slept, he ordered all the ships to be set alight. The next day he told them: 'You now have a choice: Either you fight to win or you die.' By removing the option of retreat, he switched their focus to the only thing that mattered: the battle. Spanish conquistador Cortés used the same motivational trick in the sixteenth century. After landing on the east coast of Mexico, he sank his own ship.

Xiang Yu and Cortés are exceptions. We mere mortals do everything we can to keep open the maximum number of options. Psychology professors Dan Ariely and Jiwoong Shin demonstrated the strength of this instinct using a computer game. Players started with 100 points, and on the screen in front of them, three doors appeared – a red one, a blue one and a green one. Opening a door cost a point, but for every room they entered, they could accrue more points. The players reacted logically: they found the most fruitful room, and holed up there for the whole session. Ariely and Shin then changed the rules. If doors were not opened within twelve moves, they started shrinking on the screen and eventually vanished. Players now rushed from door to door to secure access to all potential treasure troves. All this unproductive scrambling meant they scored 15% fewer points than in the previous game. The organisers then added another twist: opening doors now cost three points. The same anxiety kicked in: players frittered away their points trying to keep all doors open. Even when the subjects learned how many points were hidden in each room, nothing changed. Sacrificing options was a price they were not willing to pay.

Why do we act so irrationally? Because the downside to such behaviour is not always apparent. In the financial markets, things are clear: a financial option on a security always costs something. There is no such thing as a free option, but in most other realms, options seem to be free. This is an illusion, however. They also come at a price, but the price tag is often hidden and intangible: each decision costs mental energy and eats up precious time for thinking and living. CEOs who examine every possible expansion option often choose none in the end. Companies that aim to address all customer segments end up addressing no one. Salespeople who chase every single lead close no deals.

We are obsessed with having as many irons as possible in the fire, ruling nothing out and being open to everything. However, this can easily destroy success. We must learn to close doors. A business strategy is primarily a statement on what *not* to engage in. Adopt a life strategy similar to a corporate strategy: write down what *not* to pursue in your life. In other words, make calculated decisions to disregard certain possibilities and when an option shows up, test it against your not-to-pursue list. It will not only keep you from trouble but also save you lots of thinking time. Think hard once and then just consult your list instead of having to make up your mind whenever a new door cracks open. Most doors are not worth going through, even when the handle seems to turn so effortlessly.

See also **Sunk Cost Fallacy** (ch. 5); **Action Bias** (ch. 43)

69

DISREGARD THE BRAND NEW

Neomania

How will the world look in fifty years? What will your everyday life be like? With which items will you surround yourself?

People who pondered this question fifty years ago had fanciful notions of how 'the future' would look: highways in the skies. Cities that resemble glass worlds. Bullet trains winding between gleaming skyscrapers. We would live in plastic capsules, work in underwater cities, vacation on the moon and consume everything in pill form. We wouldn't conceive offspring any more; instead we would choose children from a catalogue. Our best friends would be robots, death would be cured and we would have exchanged our bikes for jetpacks long ago.

But hang on a second. Take a look around. You're sitting in a chair, an invention from ancient Egypt. You wear pants, developed about 5,000 years ago and adapted by Germanic tribes around 750 B.C. The idea behind your leather shoes comes from the last ice age. Your bookshelves are made of wood, one of the oldest building materials in the world. At dinnertime, you use a fork, a well-known 'killer app' from Roman times, to shovel chunks of dead animals and plants into your mouths. Nothing has changed.

So, how will the world look in fifty years? In his book *Antifragile*, Nassim Taleb gives us a clue: assume that most of the technology that has existed for the past fifty years will serve us for another half-century. And assume that recent technology will be passé in a few years' time. Why? Think of these inventions as if they were species: whatever has held its own throughout centuries of innovation will probably continue to do so in the future, too. Old technology has proven itself; it possesses an inherent logic even if we do not always understand it. If something has endured for epochs, it must be worth its salt. You can take this to heart the next time you are in a strategy meeting. Fifty years into the future will look a lot like today. Of course, you will witness the birth of many flashy gadgets and magic contraptions. But most will be short-lived.

When contemplating the future, we place far too much emphasis on flavour-of-the-month inventions and the latest 'killer apps', while underestimating the role of traditional technology. In the 1960s, space travel was all the rage, so we imagined ourselves on school trips to Mars. In the 1970s, plastic was in, so we mulled over how we would furnish our see-through houses. Taleb, who uses above-mentioned examples of new and old technologies, coined a word for this: *neomania*, the mania for all things shiny and new.

In the past, I sympathised with so-called 'early adopters', the breed of people who cannot survive without the latest iPhone. I thought they were ahead of their time. Now I regard them as irrational and suffering from a kind of sickness: *neomania*. To them, it is of minor importance if an invention provides tangible benefits; novelty matters more.

So, don't go out on a limb when forecasting the future. Stanley Kubrick's cult movie, *2001: A Space Odyssey*, illustrates why you shouldn't. Made in 1968, the movie predicted that, at the turn of the millennium, the U.S. would have a thousand-strong colony on the moon and that PanAm would operate the commuter flights there and back. With this fanciful forecast in mind, I suggest this rule of thumb: whatever has survived for X years will last another X years. Taleb wagers that the 'bullshit filter of history' will sort the gimmicks from the game-changers. And that's one bet I'm willing to back.

See also **Hedonic Treadmill** (ch. 46)

70

WHY PROPAGANDA WORKS

Sleeper Effect

During World War II, every nation produced propaganda movies. These were devised to fill the population, especially soldiers, with enthusiasm for their country and, if necessary, to bolster them to lay down their lives. The U.S. spent so much money on propaganda that the war department decided to find out whether the expense was really worth it. A number of studies were carried out to investigate how the movies affected regular soldiers. The result was disappointing: they did not intensify the privates' enthusiasm for war in the slightest.

Was it because they were poorly made? Hardly. Rather, the soldiers were aware that the movies were propaganda, which discredited their message even before they were rolling. Even if the movie argued a point reasonably or managed to stir the audience, it didn't matter; its content was deemed hollow from the outset and dismissed.

Nine weeks later, something unexpected happened. The psychologists measured the soldiers' attitudes a second time. The result: whoever had seen the movie expressed much more support for the war than those who had not viewed it. Apparently, propaganda did work after all!

The scientists were baffled, especially since they knew that an argument's persuasiveness decreased over time. It has a half-life like a radioactive substance. Surely you have experienced this yourself: let's say you read an article on the benefits of gene therapy. Immediately after reading it you are a zealous convert, but after a few weeks, you don't really remember why. More time passes until, finally, only a tiny fraction of enthusiasm remains.

Amazingly, just the opposite is true for propaganda. If it strikes a chord with someone, this influence will only increase over time. Why? Psychologist Carl Hovland, who led the study for the war department, named this phenomenon the *sleeper effect*. To date, the best explanation is that, in our memories, the *source* of the argument fades faster than the argument. In other words, your brain quickly forgets where the information came from (e.g. from the department of propaganda). Meanwhile, the message itself (i.e., war is necessary and noble) fades only slowly or even endures. Therefore, any knowledge that stems from an untrustworthy source gains credibility over time. The discrediting force melts away faster than the message does.

In the U.S., elections increasingly revolve around nasty advertisements, in which candidates seek to tarnish each another's record or reputation. However, by law, each political ad must disclose its sponsor at the end so that it is clearly distinguishable as an electioneering message. However, countless studies show that the *sleeper effect* does its job here, too, especially among undecided voters. The messenger fades from memory; the ugly accusations persevere.

I've often wondered why advertising works at all. Any logical person must recognise ads for what they are, and suitably categorise and disqualify them. But even you as a discerning and intelligent reader won't always succeed at this. It's quite possible that, after a few weeks, you won't remember if you picked up certain information from a well-researched article or from a tacky advertorial.

How can you thwart the *sleeper effect*? First, don't accept any unsolicited advice, even if it seems well meant. Doing so, you protect yourself to a certain degree from manipulation. Second, avoid ad-contaminated sources like the plague. How fortunate we are that books are (still) ad-free! Third, try to remember the source of every argument you encounter. Whose opinions are these? And why do they think that way? Probe the issue like an investigator would: *cui bono*? Who benefits? Admittedly, this is a lot of work and will slow down your decision-making. But it will also refine it.

See also **Framing** (ch. 42); **Primacy and Recency Effects** (ch. 73); **News Illusion** (ch. 99)

71

WHY IT'S NEVER JUST
A TWO-HORSE RACE

Alternative Blindness

You leaf through a brochure that gushes about the benefits of the university's MBA degree. Your gaze sweeps over photos of the ivy-covered campus and the ultra-modern sports facilities. Sprinkled throughout are images of smiling students from various ethnic backgrounds with an emphasis on young women, young Chinese and young Indian go-getters. On the last page you come to an overview that illustrates the financial value of an MBA. The $100,000 fee is easily offset by the statistical extra income that graduates earn before they retire: $400,000 – *after* taxes. Who wouldn't want to be up $300,000? It's a no-brainer.

Wrong. Such an argument hides not one, but four fallacies. First, we have the *swimmer's body illusion*: MBA programmes attract career-oriented people who will probably earn above-average salaries at some stage of their careers, even without the extra qualification of an MBA. The second fallacy: an MBA takes two years. During this time you can expect a loss of earnings – say, $100,000. So in fact, the MBA costs $200,000, not $100,000. That amount, if invested well, could easily exceed the additional income that the brochure promises. Third, to estimate earnings that are more than thirty years away is idiotic. Who knows what will happen over the next three decades? Finally, other alternatives exist. You are not stuck between 'do an MBA' and 'don't do an MBA'. Perhaps you can find a different programme that costs significantly less and also represents a shot in the arm for your career. This fourth misconception interests me the most. Let's call it *alternative blindness*: we systematically forget to compare an existing offer with the next-best alternative.

Here's an example from the world of finance. Suppose you have a little money in your savings account and you ask your investment broker for advice. He proposes a bond that will earn you 5% interest. 'That's much better than the 1% you get with your savings account,' he points out. Does it make sense to buy the bond? We don't know. It's wrong to consider just these two options. To assess your options properly, you would have to compare the bond with all other investment options and then select the best. This is how top investor Warren Buffett does things: 'Each deal we measure against the second-best deal that is available at any given time – even if it means doing more of what we are already doing.'

Unlike Warren Buffett, politicians often fall victim to *alternative blindness*. Let's say your city is planning to build a sports arena on a vacant plot of land. Supporters argue that such an arena would benefit the population much more than an empty lot – both emotionally and financially. But this comparison is wrong. They should compare the construction of the sports arena with all other ideas that become impossible due to its construction – for example, building a school, a performing arts centre, a hospital or an incinerator. They could also sell the land, and invest the proceeds or reduce the city's debt.

And you? Do you often overlook the alternatives? Let's say your doctor discovers a tumour that will kill you in five years. He proposes a complicated operation, which, if successful, removes the tumour completely. However, this procedure is highly risky with a survival rate of just 50%. How do you decide? You weigh up your choices: certain death in five years or a 50% chance of dying next week. *Alternative blindness*! Perhaps there is a variant of the invasive surgery that your hospital doesn't offer, but a hospital across town does. This invasive surgery might not remove the tumour altogether, just slow its growth, but is much safer and gives you an extra ten years. And who knows, maybe during these ten years a more sophisticated therapy for eradicating tumours will be made available.

The bottom line: if you have trouble making a decision, remember that the choices are broader than 'no surgery' or 'highly risky surgery'. Forget about the rock and the hard place, and open your eyes to the other, superior alternatives.

See also **Paradox of Choice** (ch. 21); **Swimmer's Body Illusion** (ch. 2)

72

WHY WE TAKE AIM AT YOUNG GUNS

Social Comparison Bias

As one of my books reached number one on the bestseller list, my publisher asked me for a favour. An acquaintance's title was on the verge of entering the top ten list, and the publisher was convinced that a testimonial from me would give it the necessary push.

It always amazes me that these little testimonials work at all. Everyone knows that only favourable comments end up on a book's jacket. (The book you hold in your hands is no exception.) A rational reader should ignore the praise, or at least consider it alongside the criticism, which is always available, albeit in different places. Nevertheless, I've written plenty of testimonials for other books, but they were never for rival titles. I hesitated: wouldn't writing a blurb be cutting off my nose to spite my face? Why should I help someone who might soon vie with me for the top slot? As I pondered the question, I realised *social comparison bias* had kicked in – that is, the tendency to withhold assistance to people who might outdo you, even if you look like a fool in the long run.

Book testimonials are a harmless example of the *social comparison bias*. However, the phenomenon has reached toxic levels in academia. Every scientist's goal is to publish as many articles as possible in the most prestigious scientific journals. Over time, you make a name for yourself, and soon editors ask you to assess other scientists' submissions. In the end, often just two or three experts decide what gets published in a particular field. Taking this into account, what happens if a young researcher sends in an earth-shattering paper that turns the entire department on its head and threatens to knock them off their thrones? They will be especially rigorous when evaluating the article. That's *social comparison bias* hard at work.

The psychologist Stephen Garcia and his fellow researchers describe the case of a Nobel laureate who prevented a promising young colleague from applying for a job at 'his' university. This may seem judicious in the short term, but in the long run, it is counterproductive. What happens when that young prodigy joins another research group and applies his acumen there – most likely preventing the old institution from maintaining its world-class status? Garcia suggests that *social comparison bias* may well be the reason why hardly any research groups remain at the top for many years in succession.

The *social comparison bias* is also a cause for concern with start-up companies. Guy Kawasaki was 'chief evangelist' at Apple for four years. Today he is a venture capitalist and advises entrepreneurs. Kawasaki says: 'A-players hire people even better than themselves. It's clear, though, that B-players hire C-players so they can feel superior to them, and C-players hire D-players. If you start hiring B-players, expect what Steve [Jobs] called "the bozo explosion" to happen in your organisation.' In other words, start hiring B-players and you end up with Z-players. Recommendation: hire people who are better than you, otherwise you soon preside over a pack of underdogs. The so-called *Duning–Kruger effect* applies to such Z-players: the inept are gifted at overlooking the extent of their incompetence. They suffer from illusory superiority, which leads them to make even more thinking errors, thus creating a vicious cycle that erodes the talent pool over time.

While his school was closed due to an outbreak of plague in 1666–7, 25-year-old Isaac Newton showed his professor, Isaac Barrow, what research he was conducting in his spare time. Barrow immediately gave up his job as a professor and became a student of Newton. What a noble gesture. What ethical behaviour. When was the last time you heard of a professor vacating his post in favour of a better candidate? And when was the last time you read about a CEO clearing out his desk when he realised that one of his 20,000 employees could do a better job?

In conclusion: do you foster individuals more talented than you? Admittedly, in the short term the preponderance of stars can endanger your status, but in the long run, you can only profit from their contributions. Others will overtake you at some stage anyway. Until then, you should get in the up-and-comers' good books – and learn from them. This is why I wrote the testimonial in the end.

See also **Envy** (ch. 86); **Contrast Effect** (ch. 10)

73

WHY FIRST IMPRESSIONS DECEIVE

Primacy and Recency Effects

Allow me to introduce you to two men, Alan and Ben. Without thinking about it too long, decide who you prefer. Alan is smart, hard-working, impulsive, critical, stubborn and jealous. Ben, however, is jealous, stubborn, critical, impulsive, hard-working and smart. Who would you prefer to get stuck in an elevator with? Most people choose Alan, even though the descriptions are exactly the same. Your brain pays more attention to the first adjectives in the lists, causing you to identify two different personalities. Alan is smart and hard-working. Ben is jealous and stubborn. The first traits outshine the rest. This is called the *primacy effect*.

If it were not for the *primacy effect*, people would refrain from decking out their headquarters with luxuriously appointed entrance halls. Your lawyer would feel happy turning up to meet you in worn-out sneakers rather than beautifully polished designer Oxfords.

The *primacy effect* triggers practical errors too. Nobel laureate Daniel Kahneman describes how he used to grade examination papers at the beginning of his professorship. He did it as most teachers do – in order: student 1 followed by student 2 and so on. This meant that students who answered the first questions flawlessly endeared themselves to him, thus affecting how he graded the remaining parts of their exams. So, Kahneman switched methods and began to grade the individual questions in batches – all the answers to question one, then the answers to question two, and so forth. Thus, he cancelled out the *primacy effect*.

Unfortunately, this trick is not always replicable. When recruiting a new employee, for example, you run the risk of hiring the person who makes the best first impression. Ideally, you would set up all the candidates in order and let them answer the same question one after the other.

Suppose you sit on the board of a company. A point of discussion is raised – a topic on which you have not yet passed judgement. The first opinion you hear will be crucial to your overall assessment. The same applies to the other participants, a fact that you can exploit: if you have an opinion, don't hesitate to air it first. This way, you will influence your colleagues more and draw them over to your side. If, however, you are chairing the committee, always ask members' opinions in random order so that no one has an unfair advantage.

The *primacy effect* is not always the culprit; the contrasting *recency effect* matters as well. The more recent the information, the better we remember it. This occurs because our short-term memory file drawer, as it were, contains very little extra space. When a new piece of information gets filed, an older piece of information is discarded to make room.

When does the *primacy effect* supersede the *recency effect*, or vice versa? If you have to make an immediate decision based on a series of 'impressions' (such as characteristics, exam answers etc.), the *primacy effect* weighs heavier. But if the series of impressions was formed some time ago, the *recency effect* dominates. For instance, if you listened to a speech a few weeks ago, you will remember the final point or punchline more clearly than your first impressions.

In conclusion: first and last impressions dominate, meaning that the content sandwiched between has only a weak influence. Try to avoid evaluations based on first impressions. They will deceive you, guaranteed, in one way or another. Try to assess all aspects impartially. It's not easy, but there are ways around it. For example, in interviews, I jot down a score every five minutes and calculate the average afterward. This way, I make sure that the 'middle' counts just as much as hello and goodbye.

See also **Illusion of Attention** (ch. 88); **Sleeper Effect** (ch. 70); **Salience Effect** (ch. 83)

74

WHY YOU CAN'T BEAT HOME-MADE

Not-Invented-Here Syndrome

My cooking skills are quite modest, and my wife knows it. However, every now and then I concoct a dish that could pass for edible. A few weeks ago, I bought some sole. Determined to escape the monotony of familiar sauces, I devised a new one – a daring combination of white wine, pureed pistachio nuts, honey, grated orange peel and a dash of balsamic vinegar. Upon tasting it, my wife slid her baked sole to the edge of the plate and began to scrape off the sauce, smiling ruefully as she did so. I, on the other hand, didn't think it was bad at all. I explained to her in detail what a bold creation she was missing, but her expression stayed the same.

Two weeks later, we were having sole again. This time my wife did the cooking. She prepared two sauces: the first her tried-and-true *beurre blanc*, and the other a new recipe from a top French chef. The second tasted horrible. Afterward, she confessed that it was not a French recipe at all, but a Swiss one: my masterpiece from two weeks before! She had caught me out. I was guilty of the *Not-Invented-Here syndrome* (*NIH syndrome*), which fools us into thinking anything we create ourselves is unbeatable.

NIH syndrome causes you to fall in love with your own ideas. This is valid not only for fish sauces, but also for all kinds of solutions, business ideas and inventions. Companies tend to rate home-grown ideas as far more important than those from outsiders, even if, objectively, this is not the case. I recently had lunch with the CEO of a company that specialises in software for health insurance firms. He told me how difficult it is to sell his software to potential customers, even though his firm is the market leader in terms of service, security and functionality. Most insurers are convinced that the best solution is what they have crafted themselves in-house over the past thirty years. Another CEO told me how hard it is to get his staff in the company's headquarters to accept solutions proposed from far-flung subsidiaries.

When people collaborate to solve problems and then evaluate these ideas themselves, *NIH syndrome* will inevitably exert an influence. Thus, it makes sense to split teams into two groups. The first group generates ideas; the second rates them. Then they swap: the second team comes up with ideas and the first team rates them. We tend to rate our own business ideas as more successful than other people's concepts. This self-confidence forms the basis of thriving entrepreneurship, but also explains start-ups' frequently miserable returns.

This is how psychologist Dan Ariely measured the *NIH syndrome*. Writing in his blog at the *New York Times*, Ariely asked readers to provide solutions to six issues, such as 'How can cities reduce water consumption without limiting it by law?' The readers had to make suggestions, and also assess the feasibility of all the ideas proposed. They also had to specify how much of their time and money they would invest in each idea. Finally, they were limited to using a set list of fifty words, ensuring that everyone gave more or less the same answers. Despite this, the majority rated their own responses as more important and applicable than the others, even though the submissions were virtually identical.

On a societal level, *NIH syndrome* has serious consequences. We overlook shrewd ideas simply because they come from other cultures. In Switzerland, where each state or 'canton' has certain powers, one tiny canton never approved women's suffrage; it took a federal court ruling in 1990 to change the law – a startling case of *NIH*. Or consider the modern traffic roundabout, with its clear yield requirements, that was designed by British transport engineers in the 1960s and implemented throughout the U.K. It took another thirty years full of oblivion and resistance until this obvious traffic decongestant found its way in the U.S. and continental Europe. Today France alone has more than 30,000 roundabouts – which the French now probably falsely attribute to the designer of the Place de l'Étoile.

In conclusion: we are drunk on our own ideas. To sober up, take a step back every now and then to examine their quality in hindsight. Which of your ideas from the past ten years were truly outstanding? Exactly.

See also **Introspection Illusion** (ch. 67); **Endowment Effect** (ch. 23); **Self-Serving Bias** (ch. 45); **False-Consensus Effect** (ch. 77)

75

HOW TO PROFIT FROM
THE IMPLAUSIBLE

The Black Swan

'All swans are white.' For centuries, this statement was watertight. Every snowy specimen corroborated this. A swan in a different colour? Unthinkable. That was until the year 1697, when Willem de Vlamingh saw a black swan for the first time during an expedition to Australia. Since then, black swans have become symbols of the improbable.

You invest money in the stock market. Year in, year out, the Dow Jones rises and falls a little. Gradually, you grow accustomed to this gentle up and down. Then, suddenly, a day like 19 October 1987 comes around and the stock market tumbles 22%. With no warning. This event is a Black Swan, as described by Nassim Taleb in his book with the same title.

A *Black Swan* is an unthinkable event that massively affects your life, your career, your company, your country. There are positive and negative *Black Swans*. The meteorite that flattens you, Sutter's discovery of gold in California, the collapse of the Soviet Union, the invention of the transistor, the Internet browser, the overthrow of Egyptian dictator Mubarak or another encounter that upturns your life completely – all are *Black Swans*.

Think what you like of former U.S. secretary of defence Donald Rumsfeld, but at a press conference in 2002, he expressed a philosophical thought with exceptional clarity when he offered this observation: there are things we know ('known facts'), there are things we do not know ('known unknowns') and there are things that we do not know that we do not know ('unknown unknowns').

How big is the universe? Does Iran have nuclear weapons? Does the Internet make us smarter or dumber? These are 'known unknowns'. With enough effort, we can hope to answer these one day. Unlike the 'unknown unknowns'. No one foresaw Facebook mania ten years ago. It is a *Black Swan*.

Why are *Black Swans* important? Because, as absurd as it may sound, they are cropping up more and more frequently and they tend to become more consequential. Though we can continue to plan for the future, *Black Swans* often destroy our best-laid plans. Feedback loops and non-linear influences interact and cause unexpected results. The reason: our brains are designed to help us hunt and gather. Back in the Stone Age, we hardly ever encountered anything truly extraordinary. The deer we chased was sometimes a bit faster or slower, sometimes a little bit fatter or thinner. Everything revolved around a stable mean.

Today is different. With one breakthrough, you can increase your income by a factor of 10,000. Just ask Larry Page, Usain Bolt, George Soros, J.K. Rowling or Bono. Such fortunes did not exist previously; peaks of this size were unknown. Only in the most recent of human history has this been possible – hence our problem with extreme scenarios. Since probabilities cannot fall below zero, and our thought processes are prone to error, you should assume that everything has an above-zero probability.

So, what can be done? Put yourself in situations where you can catch a ride on a positive *Black Swan* (as unlikely as that is). Become an artist, inventor or entrepreneur with a scaleable product. If you sell your time (e.g. as an employee, dentist or journalist), you are waiting in vain for such a break. But even if you feel compelled to continue as such, avoid surroundings where negative *Black Swans* thrive. This means: stay out of debt, invest your savings as conservatively as possible and get used to a modest stand-ard of living – no matter whether your big breakthrough comes or not.

See also **Ambiguity Aversion** (ch. 80); **Forecast Illusion** (ch. 40); **Alternative Paths** (ch. 39); **Expectations** (ch. 62)

76

KNOWLEDGE IS NON-TRANSFERABLE

Domain Dependence

Writing books about clear thinking brings with it many pluses. Business leaders and investors invite me to give talks for good money. (Incidentally, this is in itself poor judgement on their part: books are much cheaper.) At a medical conference, the following happened to me. I was speaking about *base-rate neglect* and illustrated it with a medical example: in a 40-year-old patient, stabbing chest pain may (among other things) indicate heart problems, or it may indicate stress. Stress is much more frequent (with a higher base rate), so it is advisable to test the patient for this first. All this is very reasonable and the doctors understood it intuitively. But when I used an example from economics, most faltered.

The same thing happens when I speak in front of investors. If I illustrate fallacies using financial examples, most catch on immediately. However, if I take instances from biology, many are lost. The conclusion: insights do not pass well from one field to another. This effect is called *domain dependence*.

In 1990, Harry Markowitz received the Nobel Prize for Economics for his theory of 'portfolio selection'. It describes the optimum composition of a portfolio, taking into account both risk and return prospects. When it came to Markowitz's own portfolio – how he should allot his savings in stocks and bonds – he simply opted for 50/50 distribution: half in shares, the other half in bonds. The Nobel Prize winner was incapable of applying his ingenious process to his own affairs. A blatant case of *domain dependence*. He failed to transfer knowledge from the academic world to the private sphere.

A friend of mine is a hopeless adrenaline junkie, scaling overhanging cliffs with his bare hands and launching himself off mountains in a wingsuit. He explained to me last week why starting a business is dangerous: bankruptcy can never be ruled out. 'Personally, I'd rather be bankrupt than dead,' I replied. He didn't appreciate my logic.

As an author, I realise just how difficult it is to transfer skills to a new area. For me, devising plots for my novels and creating characters are a cinch. A blank, empty page doesn't daunt me. It's quite a different story with, say, an empty apartment. When it comes to interior decor, I can stand in the room for hours, hands in my pockets, devoid of one single idea.

Business is teeming with *domain dependence*. A software company recruits a successful consumer-goods salesman. The new position blunts his talents; transferring his sales skills from products to services is exceedingly difficult. Similarly, a presenter who is outstanding in front of small groups may well tank when his audience reaches 100 people. Or a talented marketing mind may be promoted to CEO and suddenly find that he lacks any strategic creativity.

With the Markowitz example, we saw that the transfer from the professional realm to the private realm is particularly difficult to navigate. I know CEOs who are charismatic leaders in the office and hopeless duds at home. Similarly, it would be a hard task to find a more cigarette-toting profession than the prophets of health themselves, the doctors. Police officers are twice as violent at home as civilians. Literary critics' novels get the poorest reviews. And, almost proverbially, the marriages of couples' therapists are frequently more fragile than those of their clients. Mathematics professor Persi Diaconis tells this story: 'Some years ago I was trying to decide whether or not I should move from Stanford to Harvard. I had bored my friends silly with endless discussion. Finally, one of them said, "You're one of our leading decision theorists. Maybe you should make a list of the costs and benefits and try to roughly calculate your expected utility." Without thinking, I blurted out, "Come on, Sandy, this is serious."'

What you master in one area is difficult to transfer to another. Especially daunting is the transfer from academia to real life – from the theoretically sound to the practically possible. Of course, this also counts for this book. It will be difficult to transfer the knowledge from these pages to your daily life. Even for me as the writer that transition proves to be a tough one. Book smarts doesn't transfer to street smarts easily.

See also **Déformation Professionelle** (ch. 92); **Chauffeur Knowledge** (ch. 16); **Twaddle Tendency** (ch. 57)

77

THE MYTH OF LIKE-MINDEDNESS

False-Consensus Effect

Which do you prefer: music from the 1960s or music from the 1980s? How do you think the general public would answer this question? Most people tend to extrapolate their preferences on to others. If they love the 1960s, they will automatically assume that the majority of their peers do, too. The same goes for 1980s aficionados. We frequently overestimate unanimity with others, believing that everyone else thinks and feels exactly like we do. This fallacy is called the *false-consensus effect*.

Stanford psychologist Lee Ross hit upon this in 1977. He fashioned a sandwich board emblazoned with the slogan 'Eat at Joe's' and asked randomly selected students to wear it around campus for thirty minutes. They also had to estimate how many other students would put themselves forward for the task. Those who declared themselves willing to wear the sign assumed that the majority (62%) would also agree to it. On the other hand, those who politely refused believed that most people (67%) would find it too stupid to undertake. In both cases, the students imagined themselves to be in the popular majority.

The *false-consensus effect* thrives in interest groups and political factions that consistently overrate the popularity of their causes. An obvious example is global warming. However critical you consider the issue to be, you probably believe that the majority of people share your opinion. Similarly, if politicians are confident of election, it's not just blind optimism: they cannot help overestimating their popularity.

Artists are even worse off. In 99% of new projects, they expect to achieve more success than ever before. A personal example: I was completely convinced that my novel, *Massimo Marini*, would be a resounding success. It was at least as good as my previous books, I thought, and those had done very well. But the public was of a different opinion and I was proven wrong: *false-consensus effect*.

Of course, the business world is equally prone to such false conclusions. Just because an R&D department is convinced of its product's appeal doesn't mean consumers will think the same way. Companies with tech people in charge are especially affected. Inventors fall in love with their products' sophisticated features and mistakenly believe that these will bowl customers over, too.

The *false-consensus effect* is fascinating for yet another reason. If people do not share our opinions, we categorise them as 'abnormal'. Ross's experiment also corroborated this: the students who wore the sandwich board considered those who refused to be stuck up and humourless, whereas the other camp saw the sign-wearers as idiots and attention seekers.

Perhaps you remember the fallacy of *social proof*, the notion that an idea is better the more people believe in it. Is the *false-consensus effect* identical? No. *Social proof* is an evolutionary survival strategy. Following the crowd has saved our butts more often in the past 100,000 years than striking out on our own. With the *false-consensus effect*, no outside influences are involved. Despite this, it still has a social function, which is why evolution didn't eliminate it. Our brain is not built to recognise the truth; instead its goal is to leave behind as many offspring as possible. Whoever seemed courageous and convincing (thanks to the *false-consensus effect*) created a positive impression, attracted a disproportionate amount of resources, and thus increased their chances of passing on their genes to future generations. Doubters were less sexy.

In conclusion: assume that your worldview is not borne by the public. More than that: do not assume that those who think differently are idiots. Before you distrust them, question your own assumptions.

See also **Social Proof** (ch. 4); **Not-Invented-Here Syndrome** (ch. 74)

78

YOU WERE RIGHT ALL ALONG

Falsification of History

Winston Smith, a frail, brooding, 39-year-old office employee, works in the Ministry of Truth. His job is to update old newspaper articles and documents so that they agree with new developments. His work is important. Revising the past creates the illusion of infallibility and helps the government secure absolute power.

Such historical misrepresentation, as witnessed in George Orwell's classic *1984*, is alive and well today. It may shock you but a little Winston is scribbling away in your brain, too. Worse still: whereas in Orwell's novel, he toiled unwillingly and eventually rebelled against the system, in your brain he is working with the utmost efficiency and according to your wishes and goals. He will never rise up against you. He revises your memories so effortlessly – elegantly, even – that you never notice his work. Discreet and reliable, Winston disposes of your old, mistaken views. As they vanish one by one, you start to believe you were right all along.

In 1973, U.S. political scientist Gregory Markus asked 3,000 people to share their opinions on controversial political issues, such as the legalisation of drugs. Their responses ranged from 'fully agree' to 'completely disagree'. Ten years later, he interviewed them again on the same topics, and also asked what they had replied ten years previously. The result: what they recalled disclosing in 1973 was almost identical to their present-day views – and a far cry from their original responses.

By subconsciously adjusting past views to fit present ones, we avoid any embarrassing proof of our fallibility. It's a clever coping strategy, because no matter how tough we are, admitting mistakes is an emotionally difficult task. But this is preposterous. Shouldn't we let out a whoop of joy every time we realise we are wrong? After all, such admissions would ensure we will never make the same mistake twice and have essentially taken a step forward. But we do not see it that way.

So does this mean our brains contain no accurately etched memories? Surely not! After all, you can recall the exact moment when you met your partner as if it were captured in a photo. And you can remember exactly where you were on 11 September 2001 when you learned of the terrorist attack in New York, right? You recall to whom you were speaking and how you felt. Your memories of 9/11 are extraordinarily vivid and detailed. Psychologists call these *flashbulb memories*: they feel as incontestable as photographs.

They are not. *Flashbulb memories* are as flawed as regular recollections. They are the product of reconstruction. Ulrich Neisser, one of the pioneers in the field of cognitive science, investigated them. In 1986, the day after the explosion of the *Challenger* space shuttle, he asked students to write essays detailing their reactions. Three years later, he interviewed them again. Less than seven per cent of the new data correlated with the initial submissions. In fact, 50% of the recollections were incorrect in two-thirds of the points, and 25% failed to match even a single detail. Neisser took one of these conflicting papers and presented it to its owner. Her answer: 'I know it's my handwriting, but I couldn't have written this.' The question remains: why do *flashbulb memories* feel so real? We don't know yet.

It is safe to assume that half of what you remember is wrong. Our memories are riddled with inaccuracies, including the seemingly flawless *flashbulb memories*. Our faith in them can be harmless – or lethal. Consider the widespread use of eyewitness testimony and police line-ups to identify criminals. To trust such accounts without additional investigation is reckless, even if the witnesses are adamant that they would easily recognise the perpetrator again.

See also **Hindsight Bias** (ch. 14); **Story Bias** (ch. 13); **Fallacy of the Single Cause** (ch. 97)

79

WHY YOU IDENTIFY WITH YOUR FOOTBALL TEAM

In-Group Out-Group Bias

When I was a child, a typical wintry Sunday looked like this: my family sat in front of the TV watching a ski race. My parents cheered for the Swiss skiers and wanted me to do the same. I didn't understand the fuss. First, why zoom down a mountain on two planks? It makes as little sense as hopping up the mountain on one leg, while juggling three balls and stopping every 100 feet to hurl a log as far as possible. Second, how can one-hundredth of a second count as a difference? Common sense would say that if people are that close together, they are equally good skiers. Third, why should I identify with the Swiss skiers? Was I related to any of them? I didn't think so. I didn't even know what they thought or read, and if I lived a few feet over the Swiss border, I would probably (have to) cheer for another team altogether.

This brings us to the question: does identifying with a group – a sports team, an ethnicity, a company, a state – represent flawed thinking?

Over thousands of years, evolution has shaped every behavioural pattern, including attraction to certain groups. In times past, group membership was vital. Fending for yourself was close to impossible. As people began to form alliances, all had to follow suit. Individuals stood no chance against collectives. Whoever rejected membership or got expelled forfeited their place not only in the group, but also in the gene pool. No wonder we are such social animals – our ancestors were, too.

Psychologists have investigated different group effects. These can be neatly categorised under the term *in-group-out-group bias*. First, groups often form based on minor, even trivial, criteria. With sports affiliations, a random birthplace suffices, and in business it is where you work. To test this, the British psychologist Henri Tajfel split strangers into groups, tossing a coin to choose who went to which group. He told the members of one group it was because they all liked a particular type of art. The results were impressive: although A) they were strangers, B) they were allocated a group at random and C) they were far from art connoisseurs, the group members found each other more agreeable than members of other groups. Second, you perceive people outside your own group to be more similar than they actually are. This is called the *out-group homogeneity bias*. Stereotypes and prejudices stem from it. Have you ever noticed that, in science-fiction movies, only the humans have different cultures and the aliens do not? Third, since groups often form on the basis of common values, group members receive a disproportionate amount of support for their own views. This distortion is dangerous, especially in business: it leads to the infamous organisational blindness.

Family members helping one another out is understandable. If you share half your genes with your siblings, you are naturally interested in their well-being. But there is such a thing as 'pseudo-kinship', which evokes the same emotions without blood relationship. Such feelings can lead to the most senseless cognitive error of all: laying down your life for a random group – also known as going to war. It is no coincidence that 'motherland' suggests kinship. And it's not by chance that the goal of any military training is to forge soldiers together as 'brothers'.

In conclusion: prejudice and aversion are biological responses to anything foreign. Identifying with a group has been a survival strategy for hundreds of thousands of years. Not any longer; identifying with a group distorts your view of the facts. Should you ever be sent to war, and you don't agree with its goals, desert.

See also **Social Proof** (ch. 4); **Groupthink** (ch. 25)

80

THE DIFFERENCE BETWEEN RISK AND UNCERTAINTY

Ambiguity Aversion

Two boxes. Box A contains 100 balls: 50 red and 50 black. Box B also holds 100 balls, but you don't know how many are red and how many black. If you reach into one of the boxes without looking and draw out a red ball, you win $100. Which box will you choose: A or B? The majority will opt for A.

Let's play again, using exactly the same boxes. This time, you win $100 if you draw out a *black* ball. Which box will you go for now? Most likely you'll choose A again. But that's illogical! In the first round, you assumed that B contained fewer red balls (and more black balls), so, rationally, you would have to opt for B this time around.

Don't worry; you're not alone in this error – quite the opposite. This result is known as the *Ellsberg Paradox* – named after Daniel Ellsberg, a former Harvard psychologist. (As a side note, he later leaked the top-secret Pentagon Papers to the press, leading to the downfall of President Nixon.) The *Ellsberg Paradox* offers empirical proof that we favour known probabilities (box A) over unknown ones (box B).

Thus we come to the topics of risk and uncertainty (or ambiguity) and the difference between them. Risk means that the probabilities are known. Uncertainty means that the probabilities are unknown. On the basis of risk, you can decide whether or not to take a gamble. In the realm of uncertainty, though, it's much harder to make decisions. The terms risk and uncertainty are as frequently mixed up as cappuccino and latte macchiato – with much graver consequences. You can make calculations with risk, but not with uncertainty. The 300-year-old science of risk is called statistics. A host of professors deal with it, but not a single textbook exists on the subject of uncertainty. Because of this, we try to squeeze ambiguity into risk categories, but it doesn't really fit. Let's look at two examples: one from medicine (where it works) and one from the economy (where it does not).

There are billions of humans on earth. Our bodies do not differ dramatically. We all reach a similar height (no one will ever be 100 feet tall) and a similar age (no one will live for 10,000 years – or for only a millisecond). Most of us have two eyes, four heart valves, thirty-two teeth. Another species would consider us to be homogeneous – as similar to each other as we consider mice to be. For this reason, there are many similar diseases and it makes sense to say, for example: 'There is a 30% risk you will die of cancer.' On the other hand, the following assertion is meaningless: 'There is a 30% chance that the euro will collapse in the next five years.' Why? The economy resides in the realm of uncertainty. There are not billions of comparable currencies from whose history we can derive probabilities. The difference between risk and uncertainty also illustrates the difference between life insurance and credit default swaps. A credit default swap is an insurance policy against specific defaults, a particular company's inability to pay. In the first case (life insurance), we are in the calculable domain of risk; in the second (credit default swap), we are dealing with uncertainty. This confusion contributed to the chaos of the financial crisis in 2008. If you hear phrases such as 'the *risk* of hyperinflation is x per cent' or 'the *risk* to our equity position is y', start worrying.

To avoid hasty judgement, you must learn to tolerate ambiguity. This is a difficult task and one that you cannot influence actively. Your amygdala plays a crucial role. This is a nut-sized area in the middle of the brain responsible for processing memory and emotions. Depending on how it is built, you will tolerate uncertainty with greater ease or difficulty. This is evident not least in your political orientation: the more averse you are to uncertainty, the more conservatively you will vote. Your political views have a partial biological underpinning.

Either way, whoever hopes to think clearly must understand the difference between risk and uncertainty. Only in very few areas can we count on clear probabilities: casinos, coin tosses and probability textbooks. Often we are left with troublesome ambiguity. Learn to take it in stride.

See also **Black Swan** (ch. 75); **Neglect of Probability** (ch. 26); **Base-Rate Neglect** (ch. 28); **Availability Bias** (ch. 11); **Alternative Paths** (ch. 39)

81

WHY YOU GO WITH
THE STATUS QUO

Default Effect

In a restaurant the other day I scanned the wine list in desperation. Irouléguy? Harslevelü? Susumaniello? I'm far from an expert, but I could tell that a sommelier was trying to prove his worldliness with these selections. On the last page, I found redemption: 'Our French house wine: Réserve du Patron, Bourgogne, $52'. I ordered it right away; it couldn't be that bad, I reasoned.

I've owned an iPhone for several years now. The gadget allows me to customise everything – data usage, app synchronisation, phone encryption, even how loud I want the camera shutter to sound. How many of these have I set up so far? You guessed it: not one.

In my defence, I'm not technically challenged. Rather, I'm just another victim of the so-called *default effect*. The default setting is as warm and welcoming as a soft pillow into which we happily collapse. Just as I tend to stick with the house wine and factory cellphone settings, most people cling to the standard options. For example, new cars are often advertised in a certain colour; in every catalogue, video and ad, you see the new car in the same colour, although the car is available in a myriad of colours. The percentage of buyers who select this default colour far exceeds the percentage of car buyers who bought this particular colour in the past. Many opt for the default.

In their book, *Nudge*, economist Richard Thaler and law professor Cass Sunstein illustrate how a government can direct its citizens without unconstitutionally restricting their freedom. The authorities simply need to provide a few options – always including a default choice for indecisive individuals. This is how New Jersey and Pennsylvania presented two car-insurance policies to their inhabitants. The first policy was cheaper but waived certain rights to compensation should an accident take place. New Jersey advertised this as the standard option and most people were happy to take it. In Pennsylvania, however, the second, more expensive option was touted as the standard and promptly became the best-seller. This outcome is quite remarkable, especially when you consider that the two states' drivers cannot differ all that much in what they want covered, nor in what they want to pay.

Or consider this experiment: there is a shortage of organ donors. Only about 40% of people opt for it. Scientists Eric Johnson and Dan Goldstein asked people whether, in the event of death, they wanted to actively opt *out* of organ donation. Making donation the default option increased take-up from 40% to more than 80% of participants, a huge difference between an opt-in and an opt-out default.

The *default effect* is at work even when no standard option is mentioned. In such cases we make our past the default setting, thereby prolonging and sanctifying the status quo. People crave what they know. Given the choice of trying something new or sticking to the tried and tested option, we tend to be highly conservative even if a change would be beneficial. My bank, for example, charges an annual fee of $60 for mailing out account statements. I could save myself this amount if I downloaded the statements online. However, though the pricey (and paper-guzzling) service has bothered me for years, I still can't bring myself to get rid of it once and for all.

So where does the *status-quo bias* come from? In addition to sheer convenience, *loss aversion* plays a role. Recall that losses upset us twice as much as similar gains please us. For this reason, tasks such as renegotiating existing contracts prove very difficult. Regardless of whether these are private or professional, each concession you make weighs twice as heavy as any you receive, so such exchanges end up feeling like net losses.

Both the *default effect* and the *status-quo bias* reveal that we have a strong tendency to cling to the way things are, even if this puts us at a disadvantage. By changing the default setting, you can change human behaviour.

'Maybe we live our lives according to some grand hidden default idea,' I suggested to a dinner companion, hoping to draw him into a deep philosophical discussion. 'Maybe it just needs a little time to develop,' he said after trying the Réserve du Patron.

See also **Decision Fatigue** (ch. 53); **Paradox of Choice** (ch. 21); **Loss Aversion** (ch. 32)

82

WHY 'LAST CHANCES' MAKE US PANIC

Fear of Regret

Two stories: Paul owns shares in company A. During the year, he considered selling them and buying shares in company B. In the end, he didn't. Today he knows that if he had done so, he would have been up $1,200. Second story: George had shares in company B. During the year, he sold them and bought shares in company A. Today he also knows that if he had stuck with B, he would have netted an extra $1,200. Who feels more regret?

Regret is the feeling of having made the wrong decision. You wish someone would give you a second chance. When asked who would feel worse, 8% of respondents said Paul, whereas 92% chose George. Why? Considered objectively, the situations are identical. Both Paul and George were unlucky, picked the wrong stock, and were out of pocket by the exact same amount. The only difference: Paul already possessed the shares in A, whereas George went out and bought them. Paul was passive, George, active. Paul embodies the majority – most people leave their money lying where it is for years – and George represents the exception. It seems that whoever does not follow the crowd experiences more regret.

It is not always the one who acts who feels more regret. Sometimes, choosing not to act can constitute an exception. An example: a venerable publishing house stands alone in its refusal to publish trendy e-books. Books are made of paper, asserts the owner, and he will stick by this tradition. Shortly afterward, ten publishers go bankrupt. Nine of them attempted to launch e-book strategies and faltered. The final victim is the conventional paper-only publisher. Who will regret the series of decisions most, and who will gain the most sympathy? Right: the stoic e-grumbler.

Here is an example from Daniel Kahneman's book *Thinking, Fast and Slow*: after every plane crash, we hear the story of one unlucky person who actually wanted to fly a day earlier or later, but for some reason changed his booking at the last minute. Since he is the exception, we feel more sympathy for him than for the other 'normal' passengers who were booked on the ill-fated flight from the outset.

The *fear of regret* can make us behave irrationally. To dodge the terrible feeling in the pits of our stomachs, we tend to act conservatively, so as not to deviate from the crowd too much. No one is immune to this, not even supremely self-confident traders. Statistics show that each year on December 31 (D-day for performance reviews and bonus calculations), they tend to offload their more exotic stocks and conform to the masses. Similarly, *fear of regret* (and the *endowment effect*) prevents you from throwing away things you no longer require. You are afraid of the remorse you will feel in the unlikely event that you needed those worn-out tennis shoes after all.

The *fear of regret* becomes really irksome when combined with a 'last chance' offer. A safari brochure promises 'the last chance to see a rhino before the species is extinct'. If you never cared about seeing one before today, why would you fly all the way to Tanzania to do so now? It is irrational.

Let's say you have long dreamed of owning a house. Land is becoming scarce. Only a handful of plots with lake views are left. Three remain, then two and now just one. It's your last chance! This thought racing through your head, you give in and buy the last plot at an exorbitant price. The *fear of regret* tricked you into thinking this was a one-time offer, when in reality, real estate with a lake view will always come on the market. The sale of stunning property isn't going to stop any time soon. 'Last chances' make us panic-stricken, and the *fear of regret* can overwhelm even the most hard-headed dealmakers.

See also **Scarcity Error** (ch. 27); **Endowment Effect** (ch. 23); **Alternative Paths** (ch. 39); **Framing** (ch. 42)

83

HOW EYE-CATCHING DETAILS RENDER US BLIND

Salience Effect

Imagine the issue of marijuana has been dominating the media for the past few months. Television shows portray potheads, clandestine growers and dealers. The tabloid press prints photos of 12-year-old girls smoking joints. Broadsheets roll out the medical arguments and illuminate the societal, even philosophical aspects of the substance. Marijuana is on everyone's lips. Let's assume for a moment that smoking does not affect driving in any way. Just as anyone can wind up in an accident, a driver with a joint is also involved in a crash every now and then – purely coincidentally.

Kurt is a local journalist. One evening, he happens to drive past the scene of an accident. A car is wrapped around a tree trunk. Since Kurt has a very good relationship with the local police, he learns that they found marijuana in the back seat of the car. He hurries back to the newsroom and writes this headline: 'Marijuana Kills Yet Another Motorist'.

As stated above, we are assuming that the statistical relationship between marijuana and car accidents is zero. Thus, Kurt's headline is unfounded. He has fallen victim to the *salience effect*. *Salience* refers to a prominent feature, a standout attribute, a particularity, something that catches your eye. The *salience effect* ensures that outstanding features receive much more attention than they deserve. Since marijuana is the *salient* feature of this accident, Kurt believes that it is responsible for the crash.

A few years later, Kurt moves into business journalism. One of the largest companies in the world has just announced that it is promoting a woman to CEO. This is big news! Kurt snaps open his laptop and begins to write his commentary: the woman in question, he types, got the post simply because she is female. In truth, the promotion probably had nothing to do with gender, especially since men fill most top positions. If it were so important to have women as leaders, other companies would have acted by now. But in this news story, gender is the *salient* feature and thus it earns undue weight.

Not only journalists fall prey to the *salience effect*. We all do. Two men rob a bank and are arrested shortly after. It transpires that they are Nigerian. Although no ethnic group is responsible for a disproportionate number of bank robberies, this *salient* fact distorts our thinking. Lawless immigrants at it again, we think. If an Armenian commits rape, it is attributed to the 'Armenians' rather than other factors that also exist among Americans. Thus, prejudices form. That the vast majority of immigrants live lawful lives is easily forgotten. We always recall the undesirable exceptions – they are particularly *salient*. Therefore, whenever immigrants are involved it is the striking, negative incidents that come to mind first.

The *salience effect* influences not only how we interpret the past, but also how we imagine the future. Daniel Kahneman and his fellow researcher Amos Tversky found that we place unwarranted emphasis on *salient* information when we are forecasting. This explains why investors are more sensitive to sensational news (i.e. the dismissal of a CEO) than they are to less striking information (such as the long-term growth of a company's profits). Even professional analysts cannot always evade the *salience effect*.

In conclusion: *salient* information has an undue influence on how you think and act. We tend to neglect hidden, slow-to-develop, discrete factors. Do not be blinded by irregularities. A book with an unusual, fire-engine red jacket makes it on to the bestseller list. Your first instinct is to attribute the success of the book to the memorable cover. Don't. Gather enough mental energy to fight against seemingly obvious explanations.

See also **The Halo Effect** (ch. 38); **Primacy and Recency Effects** (ch. 73); **Confirmation Bias** (ch. 7–8); **Induction** (ch. 31); **Fundamental Attribution Error** (ch. 36); **Affect Heuristic** (ch. 66)

84

WHY MONEY IS NOT NAKED

House-Money Effect

A windy fall day in the early 1980s. The wet leaves swirled about the sidewalk. Pushing my bike up the hill to school, I noticed a strange leaf at my feet. It was big and rust-brown, and only when I bent down did I realise it was a 500-Swiss-franc bill! That was the equivalent of about $250 back then, an absolute fortune for a high school student. The money spent little time in my pocket: I soon bought myself to a top-of-the-range bike with disc brakes and Shimano gears, one of the best models around. The funny thing was, my old bike worked fine.

Admittedly, I wasn't completely broke back then: I had managed to save up a few hundred francs through mowing grass in the neighbourhood. However, it never crossed my mind to spend this hard-earned money on something so unnecessary. The most I treated myself to was a trip to the movies every now and then. It was only upon reflection that I realised how irrational my behaviour had been. Money is money after all. But we don't see it that way. Depending on how we get it, we treat it differently. Money is not naked; it is wrapped in an emotional shroud.

Two questions. You've worked hard for a year. At the end of the twelve months, you have $20,000 more in your account than you had at the beginning. What do you do? A) Leave it sitting in the bank. B) Invest it. C) Use it to make necessary improvements, such as renovating your mouldy kitchen or replacing old tyres. D) Treat yourself to a luxury cruise.

If you think like most people, you'll opt for A, B or C.

Second question. You win $20,000 in the lottery. What do you do with it? Choose from A, B, C or D above. Most people now take C or D. And of course, by doing so they exhibit flawed thinking. You can count it any way you like; $20,000 is still $20,000.

We witness similar delusions in casinos. A friend places $1,000 on the roulette table – and loses everything. When asked about this, he says: 'I didn't really gamble away $1,000. I won all that earlier.' 'But it's the same amount!' 'Not for me,' he laughs.

We treat money that we win, discover or inherit much more frivolously than hard-earned cash. The economist Richard Thaler calls this the *house-money effect*. It leads us to take bigger risks and, for this reason, many lottery winners end up worse off after they've cashed in their winnings. That old platitude – win some, lose some – is a feeble attempt to downplay real losses.

Thaler divided his students into two groups. The first group learned they had won $30 and could choose to take part in the following coin toss: if it was tails, they would win $9. If heads, they would lose $9. Seventy per cent of students opted to risk it. The second group learned they had won nothing, but that they could choose between receiving $30 or taking part in a coin toss in which heads won them $21 and tails secured $39. The second group behaved more conservatively. Only 43% were prepared to gamble – even though the expected value for both options was the same: $30.

Marketing strategists recognise the usefulness of the *house-money effect*. Online gambling sites 'reward' you with $100 credit when you sign up. Credit card companies offer the same when you fill in the application form. Airlines present you with a few thousand miles when you join their frequent flyer clubs. Phone companies give you free call credit to get you accustomed to making lots of calls. A large part of the coupon craze stems from the *house-money effect*.

In conclusion: be careful if you win money or if a business gives you something for free. Chances are you will pay it back with interest out of sheer exuberance. It's better to tear the provocative clothes from this seemingly free money. Put it in workmen's gear. Put it in your bank account or back into your own company.

See also **Endowment Effect** (ch. 23); **Scarcity Error** (ch. 27); **Loss Aversion** (ch. 32)

85

WHY NEW YEAR'S RESOLUTIONS DON'T WORK

Procrastination

A friend, a writer, someone who knows how to capture emotion in sentences – let's call him an artist – writes modest books of about 100 pages every seven years. His output is the equivalent of two lines of print per day. When asked about his miserable productivity, he says: 'Researching is just so much more enjoyable than writing.' So, he sits at his desk, surfing the web for hours on end or immersed in the most abstruse books – all in the hope of hitting upon a magnificent, forgotten story. Once he has found suitable inspiration, he convinces himself that there is no point starting until he is in the 'right mood'. Unfortunately, the right mood is a rare occurrence.

Another friend has tried to quit smoking every day for the past ten years. Each cigarette is his last. And me? My tax returns have been lying on my desk for six months, waiting to be completed. I haven't yet given up hope that they will fill themselves in.

Procrastination is the tendency to delay unpleasant but important acts: the arduous trek to the gym, switching to a cheaper insurance policy, writing thank-you letters. Even New Year's resolutions won't help you here.

Procrastination is idiotic because no project completes itself. We know that these tasks are beneficial, so why do we keep pushing them on to the back burner? Because of the time lapse between sowing and reaping. To bridge it requires a high degree of mental energy, as psychologist Roy Baumeister demonstrated in a clever experiment. He put students in front of an oven in which chocolate cookies were baking. Their delicious scent wafted around the room. He then placed a bowl filled with radishes by the oven and told the students that they could eat as many of these as they wanted, but the cookies were strictly out of bounds. He then left the students alone in the room for thirty minutes. Students in a second group were allowed to eat as many cookies as they wanted. Afterward, both groups had to solve a tough maths problem. The students who were forbidden to eat any cookies gave up on the maths problem twice as fast as those who were allowed to gorge freely on cookies. The period of self-control had drained their mental energy – or willpower – which they now needed to solve the problem. Willpower is like a battery, at least in the short term. If it is depleted, future challenges will falter.

This is a fundamental insight. Self-control is not available around the clock. It needs time to refuel. The good news: to achieve this, all you need to do is refill your blood sugar and kick back and relax.

Though eating enough and giving yourself breaks is important, the next necessary condition is employing an array of tricks to keep you on the straight and narrow. This includes eliminating distractions. When I write a novel, I turn off my Internet access. It's just too enticing to go online when I reach a knotty part. The most effective trick, however, is to set deadlines. Psychologist Dan Ariely found that dates stipulated by external authorities – for example, a teacher or the IRS – work best. Self-imposed deadlines will work only if the task is broken down step by step, with each part assigned its own due date. For this reason, nebulous New Year's resolutions are doomed to fail.

So get over yourself. *Procrastination* is irrational, but human. To fight it, use a combined approach. This is how my neighbour managed to write her doctoral thesis in three months: she rented a tiny room with neither telephone nor Internet connection. She set three dates, one for each part of the paper. She told anyone who would listen about these deadlines and even printed them on the back of her business cards. This way, she transformed personal deadlines into public commitments. At lunchtime and in the evenings, she refuelled her batteries by reading fashion magazines and sleeping a lot.

See also **Omission Bias** (ch. 44); **Planning Fallacy** (ch. 91); **Action Bias** (ch. 43); **Hyperbolic Discounting** (ch. 51); **Zeigarnik Effect** (ch. 93)

86

BUILD YOUR OWN CASTLE

Envy

Three scenarios – which would irk you the most? A) Your friends' salaries increase. Yours stays the same. B) Their salaries stay the same. Yours too. C) Their average salaries are cut. Yours is, too.

If you answered A, don't worry, that's perfectly normal: you're just another victim of the green-eyed monster.

Here is a Russian tale: a farmer finds a magic lamp. He rubs it, and out of thin air appears a genie, who promises to grant him one wish. The farmer thinks about this for a little while. Finally, he says: 'My neighbour has a cow and I have none. I hope that his drops dead.'

As absurd as it sounds, you can probably identify with the farmer. Admit it: a similar thought must have occurred to you at some point in your life. Imagine your colleague scores a big bonus and you get a gift certificate. You feel *envy*. This creates a chain of irrational behaviour: you refuse to help him any longer, sabotage his plans, perhaps even puncture the tyres of his Porsche. And you secretly rejoice when he breaks his leg skiing.

Of all the emotions, *envy* is the most idiotic. Why? Because it is relatively easy to switch off. This is in contrast to anger, sadness, or fear. 'Envy is the most stupid of vices, for there is no single advantage to be gained from it,' writes

Balzac. In short, envy is the most sincere type of flattery; other than that, it's a waste of time.

Many things spark *envy*: ownership, status, health, youth, talent, popularity, beauty. It is often confused with jealousy because the physical reactions are identical. The difference: the subject of *envy* is a thing (status, money, health etc.). The subject of jealousy is the behaviour of a third person. *Envy* needs two people. Jealousy, on the other hand, requires three: Peter is jealous of Sam because the beautiful girl next door rings him instead.

Paradoxically, with envy we direct resentments toward those who are most similar to us in age, career and residence. We don't envy businesspeople from the century before last. We don't begrudge plants or animals. We don't envy millionaires on the other side of the globe – just those on the other side of the city. As a writer, I don't envy musicians, managers or dentists, but other writers. As a CEO you envy other, bigger CEOs. As a supermodel you envy more successful supermodels. Aristotle knew this: 'Potters envy potters.'

This brings us to a classic practical error: let's say your financial success allows you to move from one of New York's grittier neighbourhoods to Manhattan's Upper East Side. In the first few weeks, you enjoy being in the centre of everything and how impressed your friends are with your new apartment and address. But soon you realise that apartments of completely different proportions surround you. You have traded in your old peer group for one that is much richer. Things start to bother you that haven't bothered you before. *Envy* and status anxiety are the consequences.

How do you curb *envy*? First, stop comparing yourself to others. Second, find your 'circle of competence' and fill it on your own. Create a niche where you are the best. It doesn't matter how small your area of mastery is. The main thing is that you are king of the castle.

Like all emotions, *envy* has its origins in our evolutionary past. If the hominid from the cave next door took a bigger share of the mammoth, it meant less for the loser. *Envy* motivated us to do something about it. *Laissez-faire* hunter-gatherers disappeared from the gene pool; in extreme cases, they died of starvation, while others feasted. We are the offspring of the envious. But, in today's world, *envy* is no longer vital. If my neighbour buys himself a Porsche, it doesn't mean that he has taken anything from me.

When I find myself suffering pangs of *envy*, my wife reminds me: 'It's OK to be envious – but only of the person you aspire to become.'

See also **Social Comparison Bias** (ch. 72); **Hedonic Treadmill** (ch. 46)

87

WHY YOU PREFER NOVELS TO STATISTICS

Personification

For eighteen years, the American media was prohibited from showing photographs of fallen soldiers' coffins. In February 2009, defence secretary Robert Gates lifted this ban and images flooded on to the Internet. Officially, family members have to give their approval before anything is published, but such a rule is unenforceable. Why was this ban created in the first place? To conceal the true costs of war. We can easily find out the number of casualties, but statistics leave us cold. People, on the other hand, especially dead people, spark an emotional reaction.

Why is this? For aeons, groups have been essential to our survival. Thus, over the past 100,000 years, we have developed an impressive sense of how others think and feel. Science calls this the 'theory of mind'. Here's an experiment to illustrate it: you are given $100 and must share it with a stranger. You can decide how it is divided up. If the other person is happy with your suggestion, the money will be divided that way. If he or she turns down your offer, you must return the $100, and no one gets anything. How do you split the sum?

It would make sense to offer the stranger very little – maybe just a dollar. After all, it's better than nothing.

However, in the 1980s, when economists began experimenting with such 'ultimatum games' (the technical term), the subjects behaved very differently: they offered the other party between 30% and 50%. Anything below 30% was considered 'unfair'. The ultimatum game is one of the clearest manifestations of the 'theory of mind': in short, we empathise with the other person.

However, with one tiny change it is possible to near-eliminate this compassion: put the players in separate rooms. When people can't see their counterparts – or, indeed, when they have never seen them – it is more difficult to simulate their feelings. The other person becomes an abstraction, and the share they are offered drops, on average, to below 20%.

In another experiment, psychologist Paul Slovic asked people for donations. One group was shown a photo of Rokia from Malawi, an emaciated child with pleading eyes. Afterward, people donated an average of $2.83 to the charity (out of $5 they were given to fill out a short survey). The second group was shown statistics about the famine in Malawi, including the fact that more than three million malnourished children were affected. The average donation dropped by 50%. This is illogical: you would think that people's generosity would grow if they knew the extent of the disaster. But we do not function like that. Statistics don't stir us; people do.

The media have long known that factual reports and bar charts do not entice readers. Hence the guideline: give the story a face. If a company features in the news, a picture of the CEO appears alongside (either grinning or grimacing, depending on the market). If a state makes the headlines, the president represents it. If an earthquake takes place, a victim becomes the face of the crisis.

This obsession explains the success of a major cultural invention: the novel. This literary 'killer app' projects personal and interpersonal conflicts on to a few individual destinies. A scholar could have written a meaty dissertation about the methods of psychological torture in Puritan New England, but instead, we still read Hawthorne's *The Scarlet Letter*. And the Great Depression? In statistical form, this is just a long series of numbers. As a family drama, in Steinbeck's *The Grapes of Wrath*, it is unforgettable.

In conclusion: be careful when you encounter human stories. Ask for the facts and the statistical distribution behind them. You can still be moved by the story, but this way, you can put it into the right context. If, however, you seek to move and motivate people for your own ends, make sure your tale is seasoned with names and faces.

See also **Story Bias** (ch. 13); **News Illusion** (ch. 99); **Linking Bias** (ch. 22)

88

YOU HAVE NO IDEA WHAT YOU ARE OVERLOOKING

Illusion of Attention

After heavy rains in the south of England, a river in a small village overflowed its banks. The police closed the ford, the shallow part of the river where vehicles cross, and diverted traffic. The crossing stayed closed for two weeks, but each day at least one car drove past the warning sign and into the rushing water. The drivers were so focused on their car's navigation systems that they didn't notice what was right in front of them.

The above observation is from cognitive psychologists Daniel Simons and Christopher Chabris. At Harvard in the 1990s, they filmed two teams of students passing basketballs back and forth. One team wore black T-shirts, the other white. The short clip, 'The Monkey Business Illusion', is available on YouTube. (Take a look before reading on.) In the video, viewers are asked to count how many times the players in white T-shirts pass the ball. Both teams move in circles, weaving in and out, passing back and forth. Suddenly, in the middle of the video, something bizarre happens: a student dressed as a gorilla walks into the centre of the room, pounds his chest and promptly disappears again. At the end, you are asked if you noticed anything unusual. Half the viewers shake their heads in astonishment. Gorilla? What gorilla?

The monkey business test is considered one of the most famous experiments in psychology and demonstrates the so-called *illusion of attention*: we are confident that we notice everything that takes place in front of us. But in reality, we often see only what we are focusing on – in this case, the passes made by the team in white. Unexpected, unnoticed interruptions can be as large and conspicuous as a gorilla.

The *illusion of attention* can be precarious, for example, when making a phone call while driving. Most of the time doing so poses no problems. The call does not negatively influence the straightforward task of keeping the car in the middle of the lane and braking when a car in front does. But as soon as an unanticipated event takes place, such as a child running across the street, your attention is too stretched to react in time. Studies show that drivers' reactions are equally slow when using a cellphone as when under the influence of alcohol or drugs. Furthermore, it does not matter whether you hold the phone with one hand, jam it between your shoulder and jaw, or use a hands-free kit: your responsiveness to unexpected events is still compromised.

Perhaps you know the expression 'the elephant in the room'. It refers to an obvious subject that nobody wants to discuss. A kind of taboo. In contrast, let us define what 'the gorilla in the room' is: a topic that is of the utmost importance and urgency, and that we absolutely need to address, but nobody knows about it.

Take the case of Swissair, a company that was so fixated on expansion that it overlooked its evaporating liquidity and went bankrupt in 2001. Or the mismanagement in the Eastern bloc that led to the fall of the Berlin Wall. Or the risks on banks' books that up until 2007 nobody paid any attention to. Such gorillas stomp around right in front of us – and we barely spot them.

It's not the case that we miss every extraordinary event. The crux of the matter is that whatever we fail to notice remains unheeded. Therefore, we have no idea what we are overlooking. This is exactly why we still cling to the dangerous illusion that we perceive everything of importance.

Purge yourself of the *illusion of attention* every now and then. Confront all possible and seemingly impossible scenarios. What unexpected events might happen? What lurks beside and behind the burning issues? What is no one addressing? Pay attention to silences as much as you respond to noises. Check the periphery, not just the centre. Think the unthinkable. Something unusual can be huge; we still may not see it. Being big and distinctive is not enough to be seen. The unusual and huge thing must be expected.

See also **Feature-Positive Effect** (ch. 95); **Confirmation Bias** (chs. 7–8); **Availability Bias** (ch. 11); **Primacy and Recency Effects** (ch. 73)

89

HOT AIR

Strategic Misrepresentation

Suppose you apply for your dream job. You buff your resumé to a shine. In the job interview, you highlight your achievements and abilities and gloss over weak points and setbacks. When they ask if you could boost sales by 30% while cutting costs by 30%, you reply in a calm voice: 'Consider it done.' Even though you are trembling inside and racking your brain about how the hell you are going to pull that off, you do and say whatever is necessary to get the job. You concentrate on wowing the interviewers; the details will follow. You know that if you give even semi-realistic answers, you'll put yourself out of the race.

Imagine you are a journalist and have a great idea for a book. The issue is on everyone's lips. You find a publisher who is willing to pay a nice advance. However, he needs to know your timeline. He removes his glasses and looks at you: 'When can I expect the manuscript? Can you have it ready in six months?' You gulp. You've never written a book in under three years. Your answer: 'Consider it done.' Of course you don't want to lie, but you know that you won't get the advance if you tell the truth. Once the contract is signed and the money is nestling in your bank account, you can always keep the publisher at bay for a while. You're a writer; you're great at making up stories!

The official term for such behaviour is *strategic misrepresentation*: the more at stake, the more exaggerated your assertions become. *Strategic misrepresentation* does not work everywhere. If your ophthalmologist promises five times in a row to give you perfect vision, but after each procedure you see worse than before, you will stop taking him seriously at some point. However, when unique attempts are involved, *strategic misrepresentation* is worth a try – in interviews, for example, as we saw above. A single company isn't going to hire you several times. It's either a yes or no.

Most vulnerable to *strategic misrepresentation* are mega-projects, where A) accountability is diffuse (for example, if the government that commissioned the project is no longer in power), B) many businesses are involved, leading to mutual finger-pointing, or C) the end date is a few years down the road.

No one knows more about large-scale projects than Oxford professor Bent Flyvbjerg. Why are cost and schedule overruns so frequent? Because it is not the best offer overall that wins; it is whichever one looks best on paper. Flyvbjerg calls this 'reverse Darwinism': whoever produces the most hot air will be rewarded with the project. However, is *strategic misrepresentation* simply brazen deceit? Yes and no. Are women who wear make-up frauds? Are men who lease Porsches to signal financial prowess liars? Yes and no. Objectively they are, but the deceit is socially acceptable, so we don't get worked up about it. The same counts for *strategic misrepresentation*.

In many cases, *strategic misrepresentation* is harmless. However, for the things that matter, such as your health or future employees, you must be on your guard. So, if you are dealing with a person (a first-rate candidate, an author or an ophthalmologist), don't go by what they claim; look at their past performance. When it comes to projects, consider the timeline, benefits and costs of similar projects, and grill anyone whose proposals are much more optimistic. Ask an accountant to pick apart the plans mercilessly. Add a clause into the contract that stipulates harsh financial penalties for cost and schedule overruns. And, as an added safety measure, have this money transferred to a secure escrow account.

See also **Overconfidence Effect** (ch. 15)

90

WHERE'S THE OFF SWITCH?

Overthinking

There was once an intelligent centipede. Sitting on the edge of a table, he looked over and saw a tasty grain of sugar across the room. Clever as he was, he started to weigh up the best route: which table leg should he crawl down – left or right – and which table leg should he crawl up? The next tasks were to decide which foot should take the first step, in which order the others should follow, and so on. He was adept at mathematics, so he analysed all the variants and selected the best path. Finally, he took the first step. However, still engrossed in calculation and contemplation, he got tangled up and stopped dead in his tracks to review his plan. In the end, he came no further and starved.

The British Open golf tournament in 1999: French golfer Jean Van de Velde played flawlessly until the final hole. With a three-shot lead, he could easily afford a double-bogey (two over par) and still win. Child's play! Entry into the big leagues was now only a matter of minutes away. All he needed to do was to play it safe. But as Van de Velde stepped up, beads of sweat began to form on his forehead. He teed off like a beginner. The ball sailed into the bushes, landing almost two hundred metres from the hole. He became increasingly nervous. The next shots were no better. He hit the ball into knee-high grass, then into the water. He took off his shoes, waded into the water and for a minute contemplated shooting from the pond. But he decided to take the penalty. He then shot into the sand. His body movements suddenly resembled those of a novice. Finally, he made it onto the green and – after a seventh attempt – into the hole. Van de Velde lost the British Open and secured a place in sporting history with his now-notorious triple-bogey.

In the 1980s, *Consumer Reports* asked experienced tasters to sample forty-five different varieties of strawberry jelly. A few years later, psychology professors Timothy Wilson and Jonathan Schooler repeated the experiment with students from the University of Washington. The results were almost identical. Both students and experts preferred the same type. But that was only the first part of Wilson's experiment. He repeated it with a second group of students who, unlike the first group, had to fill in a questionnaire justifying their ratings in detail. The rankings turned out to be completely warped. Some of the best varieties ended up at the bottom of the rankings.

Essentially, if you think too much, you cut off your mind from the wisdom of your feelings. This may sound a little esoteric – and a bit surprising coming from someone like me who strives to rid my thinking of irrationality – but it is not. Emotions form in the brain, just as crystal-clear, rational thoughts do. They are merely a different form of information processing – more primordial, but not necessarily an inferior variant. In fact, sometimes they provide the wiser counsel.

This raises the question: when do you listen to your head and when do you heed your gut? A rule of thumb might be: if it is something to do with practised activities, such as motor skills (think of the centipede, Van de Velde or mastering a musical instrument), or questions you've answered a thousand times (think of Warren Buffett's 'circle of competence'), it's better not to reflect to the last detail. It undermines your intuitive ability to solve problems. The same applies to decisions that our Stone Age ancestors faced – evaluating what was edible, who would make good friends, whom to trust. For such purposes, we have *heuristics*, mental shortcuts that are clearly superior to rational thought. With complex matters, though, such as investment decisions, sober reflection is indispensable. Evolution has not equipped us for such considerations, so logic trumps intuition.

See also **Action Bias** (ch. 43); **Information Bias** (ch. 59)

91

WHY YOU TAKE ON TOO MUCH

Planning Fallacy

Every morning, you compile a to-do list. How often does it happen that everything is checked off by the end of the day? Always? Every other day? Maybe once a week? If you are like most people, you will achieve this rare state once a month. In other words, you systematically take on too much. More than that: your plans are absurdly ambitious. Such a thing would be forgivable if you were a planning novice. But you've been compiling to-do lists for years, if not decades. Thus, you know your capabilities inside out and it's unlikely that you overestimate them afresh every day. This is not facetiousness: in other areas, you learn from experience. So why is there no learning curve when it comes to making plans? Even though you realise that most of your previous endeavours were overly optimistic, you believe in all seriousness that, today, the same workload – or more – is eminently doable. Daniel Kahneman calls this the *planning fallacy*.

In their last semesters, students generally have to write theses. The Canadian psychologist Roger Buehler and his research team asked the following of their final-year class. The students had to specify two submission dates: the first was a 'realistic' deadline and the second was a 'worst-case scenario' date. The result? Only 30% of students made the realistic deadlines. On average, the students needed 50% more time than planned – and a full seven days more than their worst-case scenario date.

The *planning fallacy* is particularly evident when people work together – in business, science and politics. Groups overestimate duration and benefits and systematically underestimate costs and risks. The conch-shaped Sydney Opera House was planned in 1957: completion was due in 1963 at a cost of $7 million. It finally opened its doors in 1973 after $102 million had been pumped in – 14 times the original estimate!

So why are we not natural-born planners? The first reason: wishful thinking. We want to be successful and achieve everything we take on. Second, we focus too much on the project and overlook outside influences. Unexpected events too often scupper our plans. This is true for daily schedules, too: your daughter swallows a fish bone. Your car battery gives up the ghost. An offer for a house lands on your desk and must be discussed urgently. There goes the plan. If you planned things even more minutely, would that be a solution? No, step-by-step preparation amplifies the *planning fallacy*. It narrows your focus even more and thus distracts you even more from anticipating the unexpected.

So what can you do? Shift your focus from internal things, such as your own project, to external factors, like similar projects. Look at the base rate and consult the past. If other ventures of the same type lasted three years and devoured $5 million, this will probably apply to your project, too – no matter how carefully you plan. And, most importantly, shortly before decisions are made, perform a so-called 'premortem' session (literally, 'before death'). The American psychologist Gary Klein recommends delivering this short speech to the assembled team: 'Imagine it is a year from today. We have followed the plan to the letter. The result is a disaster. Take five or ten minutes to write about this disaster.' The stories will show you how things might turn out.

See also **Procrastination** (ch. 85); **Forecast Illusion** (ch. 40); **Zeigarnik Effect** (ch. 93); **Groupthink** (ch. 25)

92

THOSE WIELDING HAMMERS
SEE ONLY NAILS

Déformation Professionnelle

A man takes out a loan, starts a company, and goes bankrupt shortly afterward. He falls into a depression and commits suicide.

What do you make of this story? As a business analyst, you want to understand why the business idea did not work: was he a bad leader? Was the strategy wrong, the market too small or the competition too large? As a marketer, you imagine the campaigns were poorly organised, or that he failed to reach his target audience. If you are a financial expert, you ask whether the loan was the right financial instrument. As a local journalist, you realise the potential of the story: how lucky that he killed himself! As a writer, you think about how the incident could develop into a kind of Greek tragedy. As a banker, you believe an error took place in the loan department. As a socialist, you blame the failure of capitalism. As a religious conservative, you see in this a punishment from God. As a psychiatrist, you recognise low serotonin levels. Which is the 'correct' viewpoint?

None of them. 'If your only tool is a hammer, all your problems will be nails,' said Mark Twain – a quote that sums up the *déformation professionnelle*. Charlie Munger,

Warren Buffett's business partner, named the effect the *man with the hammer tendency* after Twain: 'But that's a perfectly disastrous way to think and a perfectly disastrous way to operate in the world. So you've got to have multiple models. And the models have to come from multiple disciplines – because all the wisdom of the world is not to be found in one little academic department.'

Here are a few examples of *déformation professionnelle*: surgeons want to solve almost every medical problem with a scalpel, even if their patients could be treated with less invasive methods. Armies think of military solutions first. Engineers, structural. Trend gurus see trends in everything (incidentally, this is one of the most idiotic ways to view the world). In short: if you ask someone the crux of a particular problem, they usually link it to their own area of expertise.

So what's wrong with that? It's good if, say, a tailor sticks to what he knows. The *déformation professionnelle* becomes hazardous when people apply their specialised processes in areas where they don't belong. Surely you've come across some of these: teachers who scold their friends like students. New mothers who begin to treat their husbands like children. Or consider the omnipresent Excel spreadsheet that is featured on every computer: we use them even when it makes no sense – for example, when generating ten-year financial projections for start-ups or when comparing potential lovers we have 'sourced' from dating sites. Excel spreadsheets might well be one of the most dangerous recent inventions.

Even in his own jurisdiction, the *man with the hammer* tends to overuse it. Literary reviewers are trained to detect authors' references, symbols and hidden messages. As a novelist, I realise that literary reviewers conjure up such devices where there are none. This is not a million miles away from what business journalists do. They scour the most trivial utterings of central bank governors and somehow discover hints of fiscal policy change by parsing their words.

In conclusion: if you take your problem to an expert, don't expect the overall best solution. Expect an approach that can be solved with the expert's toolkit. The brain is not a central computer. Rather, it is a Swiss Army knife with many specialised tools. Unfortunately, our 'pocketknives' are incomplete. Given our life experiences and our professional expertise, we already possess a few blades. But to better equip ourselves, we must try to add two or three additional tools to our repertoire – mental models that are far afield from our areas of expertise. For example, over the past few years, I have begun to take a biological view of the world and have won a new understanding of complex systems. Locate your shortcomings and find suitable knowledge and methodologies to balance them. It takes about a year to internalise the most important ideas of a new field, and it's worth it: your pocketknife will be bigger and more versatile, and your thoughts sharper.

See also **Volunteer's Folly** (ch. 65); **Domain Dependence** (ch. 76); **Gambler's Fallacy** (ch. 29)

93

MISSION ACCOMPLISHED

Zeigarnik Effect

Berlin, 1927: a group of university students and professors visit a restaurant. The waiter takes order upon order, including special requests, but does not bother to write anything down. This is going to end badly, they think. But, after a short wait, all diners receive exactly what they ordered. After dinner, outside on the street, Russian psychology student Bluma Zeigarnik notices that she has left her scarf behind in the restaurant. She goes back in, finds the waiter with the incredible memory and asks him if he has seen it. He stares at her blankly. He has no idea who she is or where she sat. 'How can you have forgotten?' she asks indignantly. 'Especially with your super memory!' The waiter replies curtly: 'I keep every order in my head – until it is served.'

Zeigarnik and her mentor Kurt Lewin studied this strange behaviour and found that all people function more or less like the waiter. We seldom forget uncompleted tasks; they persist in our consciousness and do not let up, tugging at us like little children, until we give them our attention. On the other hand, once we've completed a task and checked it off our mental list, it is erased from memory.

The researcher has lent her name to this: scientists now speak of the *Zeigarnik effect*. However, in her investigation she uncovered a few untidy outliers: some people kept a completely clear head even if they had dozens of projects on the go. Only in recent years could Roy Baumeister and his research team at Florida State University shed light on this. He took students who were a few months away from their final examinations, and split them into three groups. Group 1 had to focus on a party during the current semester. Group 2 had to concentrate on the exam. Group 3 had to focus on the exam and also create a detailed study plan. Then Baumeister asked students to complete words under time pressure. Some students saw 'pa—' and filled in 'panic', while others thought of 'party' or 'Paris'. This was a clever method of finding out what was on each of their minds. As expected, group 1 had relaxed about the upcoming exam, while students in group 2 could think of nothing else. Most astonishing was the result from group 3. Although these students also had to focus on the upcoming exam, their minds were clear and free from anxiety. Further experiments confirmed this. Outstanding tasks gnaw at us only until we have a clear idea of how we will deal with them. Zeigarnik mistakenly believed that it was necessary to complete tasks to erase them from memory. But it's not; a good plan of action suffices.

David Allen, the author of a best-selling book aptly entitled *Getting Things Done*, argues that he has one goal: to have a head as clear as water. For this, you don't need to have your whole life sorted into tidy compartments. But it does mean that you need a detailed plan for dealing with the messier areas. This plan must be divided into step-by-step tasks and preferably written down. Only when this is done can your mind rest. The adjective 'detailed' is important. 'Organise my wife's birthday party' or 'find a new job' are worthless. Allen forces his clients to split such projects into twenty to fifty individual tasks.

It's worth noting that Allen's recommendation seems to fly in the face of the *planning fallacy* (chapter 91): the more detailed our planning, the more we tend to overlook factors from the periphery that will derail our projects. But here is the rub: if you want peace of mind, go for Allen's approach. If you want the most accurate estimate on cost, benefit, and duration of a project, forget your detailed plan and look up similar projects. If you want both, do both.

Fortunately, you can do all this yourself with the aid of a decidedly low-tech device. Place a notepad by your bed. The next time you cannot get to sleep, jot down outstanding tasks and how you will tackle them. This will silence the cacophony of inner voices. 'You want to find God, but you're out of cat food, so create a plan to deal with it,' says Allen. His advice is sound, even if you have already found God or have no cat.

See also **Procrastination** (ch. 85); **Planning Fallacy** (ch. 91)

94

THE BOAT MATTERS MORE
THAN THE ROWING

Illusion of Skill

Why are there so few serial entrepreneurs – business-people who start successful companies one after the other? Of course, there's Steve Jobs and Richard Branson, but they represent a tiny minority. Serial entrepreneurs account for less than one per cent of everyone who starts a company. Do they all retire to their private yachts after the first success just like Microsoft co-founder Paul Allen did? Surely not. True business people possess too much get-up-and-go to lie on a beach chair for hours on end. Is it because they can't let go and want to cosset their firms until they turn 65? No. Most founders sell their shares within ten years. Actually, you would assume that such self-starters who are blessed with talent, a good personal network and a solid reputation would be well equipped to found numerous other start-ups. So why do they stop? They didn't stop. They just failed at succeeding. Only one answer makes sense: luck plays a bigger role than skill does. No businessperson likes to hear this. When I first heard about the *illusion of skill*, my reaction was: 'What, my success was a fluke?' At first, it sounds a little offensive, especially if you worked hard to get there.

Let's take a sober look at business success. How much of it comes down to luck, and how much is the fruit of hard work and distinct talent? The question is easily misunderstood. Of course, little is achieved without talent, and nothing is achieved without hard work. Unfortunately, neither skills nor toil and trouble are the key criteria for success. They are *necessary* – but not sufficient. How do we know this? There is a very simple test: when a person is successful for a long time – more than that, when they enjoy more success in the long run compared to less qualified people – then and only then is talent the essential element. This is not the case with company founders; otherwise, the majority of successful entrepreneurs would, after the first achievement, continue to found and grow second, third and fourth start-ups.

What about corporate leaders? How important are they to the success of a company? Researchers determined a set of traits deemed to be associated with 'a strong CEO' – management procedures, strategic brilliance in the past etc. Then they measured the relationship between these behaviours on one hand, and the increase of the companies' values during the reign of these CEOs on the other hand. The result: if you compare two companies at random, in 60% of cases the stronger CEO leads the stronger company. In 40% of the cases, the weaker CEO leads the stronger company. This is only 10 percentage points more than no relationship at all. Kahneman said: 'It's hard to imagine that people enthusiastically buy books written by business leaders who are, on average, only slightly better than the norm.' Even Warren Buffett thinks nothing of CEO deification: '[. . .] A good managerial record [. . .] is far more a function of what business boat you get into than it is of how effectively you row.'

In certain areas, skill plays no role whatsoever. In his book *Thinking, Fast and Slow*, Kahneman describes his visit to an asset management company. To brief him, they sent him a spreadsheet showing the performance of each investment adviser over the past eight years. From this, a ranking was assigned to each: number 1, 2, 3 and so on in descending order. This was compiled every year. Kahneman quickly calculated the relationship between the years' rankings. Specifically, he calculated the correlation of the rankings between year 1 and year 2, between year 1 and year 3, year 1 and year 4, up until year 7 and year 8. The result: pure coincidence. Sometimes the adviser was at the very top and sometimes the very bottom. If an adviser had a great year, this was neither bolstered by previous years nor carried into subsequent years. The correlation was zero. And yet the consultants pocketed bonuses for their performance. In other words, the company was rewarding luck rather than skill.

In conclusion: certain people make a living from their abilities, such as pilots, plumbers and lawyers. In other areas, skill is necessary but not critical, as with entrepreneurs and leaders. Finally, chance is the deciding factor in a number of fields, such as in financial markets. Here, the *illusion of skill* pervades. So: give plumbers due respect and chuckle at successful financial jesters.

See also **Beginner's Luck** (ch. 49); **Survivorship Bias** (ch. 1); **Authority Bias** (ch. 9); **Overconfidence Effect** (ch. 15); **Illusion of Control** (ch. 17); **Outcome Bias** (ch. 20)

95

WHY CHECKLISTS
DECEIVE YOU

Feature-Positive Effect

Two series of numbers: the first, series A, consists of: 724, 947, 421, 843, 394, 411, 054, 646. What do these numbers have in common? Don't read on until you have an answer. It's simpler than you think: the number four features in each of them. Now examine series B: 349, 851, 274, 905, 772, 032, 854, 113. What links these numbers? Do not read further until you've figured it out. Series B is more difficult, right? Answer: none use the number six. What can you learn from this? Absence is much harder to detect than presence. In other words, we place greater emphasis on what is present than on what is absent.

Last week, while on a walk, it occurred to me that nothing hurt. It was an unexpected thought. I rarely experience pain anyway, but when I do, it is very present. But the absence of pain I rarely recognise. It was such a simple, obvious fact, it amazed me. For a moment, I was elated – until this little revelation slipped from my mind again.

At a classical recital, an orchestra performed Beethoven's Ninth Symphony. A storm of enthusiasm gripped the concert hall. During the ode in the fourth movement, tears of joy could be seen here and there. How fortunate we are that this symphony exists, I thought. But is that really true?

Would we be less happy without the work? Probably not. Had the symphony never been composed, no one would miss it. The director would receive no angry calls saying: 'Please have this symphony written and performed immediately.' In short, what exists means a lot more than what is missing. Science calls this the *feature-positive effect*.

Prevention campaigns utilise this well. 'Smoking causes lung cancer' is much more powerful than 'Not smoking leads to a life free of lung cancer.' Auditors and other professionals who employ checklists are prone to the *feature-positive effect*: outstanding tax declarations are immediately obvious because they feature on their lists. What does not appear, however, is more artistic fraud, such as the goings-on at Enron and with Bernie Madoff's Ponzi scheme. Also absent are the undertakings of 'rogue traders', such as Nick Leeson and Jerome Kerviel, to whom Barings and Société Générale fell victim. Financial vagaries of this kind are not on any checklist. And they do not have to be illegal: a mortgage bank will be on the lookout for credit risk due to a drop in the debtor's income because this appears on its list; however it will overlook the devaluation of property, say, through the construction of an incineration plant in the vicinity.

Suppose you manufacture a dubious product, such as a salad dressing with a high level of cholesterol. What do you do? On the label, you promote the twenty different vitamins in the dressing and omit the cholesterol level. Consumers won't notice its absence. And the positive, present features will make sure that they feel safe and informed.

In academia, we constantly encounter the *feature-positive effect*. The confirmation of hypotheses leads to publications and, in exceptional cases, these are rewarded with Nobel prizes. On the other hand, the falsification of a hypothesis is a lot harder to get published, and as far as I know there has never been a Nobel Prize awarded for this. However, such falsification is as scientifically valuable as confirmation. Another consequence of the effect is that we are also much more open to positive advice (do X) than to negative suggestions (forget about Y) – no matter how useful the latter may be.

In conclusion: we have problems perceiving non-events. We are blind to what does not exist. We realise if there is a war, but we do not appreciate the absence of war during peacetime. If we are healthy, we rarely think about being sick. Or, if we get off the plane in Cancun, we do not stop to notice that we did not crash. If we thought more frequently about absence, we might well be happier. But it is tough mental work. The greatest philosophical question is why does something and not *nothing* exist? Don't expect a quick answer; rather, the question itself represents a useful instrument for combating the *feature-positive effect*.

See also **Forer Effect** (ch. 64); **Confirmation Bias** (chs. 7-8); **Self-Selection Bias** (ch. 47); **Availability Bias** (ch. 11); **Illusion of Attention** (ch. 88)

96

DRAWING THE BULL'S-EYE
AROUND THE ARROW

Cherry-picking

On their websites, hotels present themselves in the very best light. They carefully select each photo, and only beautiful, majestic images make the cut. Unflattering angles, dripping pipes and drab breakfast rooms are swept under the tattered carpet. Of course, you know this is true. When you are confronted by the shabby lobby for the first time, you simply shrug your shoulders and head to the registration desk.

What the hotel did, explains Nassim Taleb, is called *cherry-picking*: showcasing the most attractive features and hiding the rest. As with the hotel experience, you approach other things with the same muted expectations: brochures for cars, real estate or law firms. You know how they work and you don't fall for them.

However, you respond differently to the annual reports of companies, foundations and government organisations. Here, you tend to expect objective depictions. You are mistaken. These bodies also *cherry-pick*: if goals are achieved, they are talked up; if they falter, they are not even mentioned.

Suppose you are the head of a department. The board invites you to present your team's state of play. How do you tackle this? You devote most of your PowerPoint slides to elaborate on the team's triumphs and throw in a token few to identify 'challenges'. Any other unmet achievements you conveniently forget.

Anecdotes are a particularly tricky sort of *cherry-picking*. Imagine you are the managing director of a company that manufactures some kind of technical device. A survey has revealed that the vast majority of customers cannot operate your gadget. It's too complicated. Now the HR manager gives his two cents, proclaiming: 'My father-in-law picked it up yesterday and figured out how to work it straight away.' How much weight would you attach to this particular cherry? Right: close to zero. To rebuff an anecdote is difficult because it is a mini-story, and we know how vulnerable our brains are to those. To prevent this, cunning leaders train themselves throughout their careers to be hypersensitive to such anecdotes and to shoot them down as soon as they are uttered.

The more elevated or elite a field is, the more we fall for *cherry-picking*. In *Antifragile*, Taleb describes how all areas of research – from philosophy to medicine to economics – brag about their results: 'Like politicians, academia is well equipped to tell us what it did for us, not what it did not – hence it shows how indispensable her methods are.' Pure *cherry-picking*. But our respect for academics is far too great for us to notice this.

Or consider the medical profession. To tell people that they should not smoke is the greatest medical contribution of the past sixty years – superior to all the research and medical advances since the end of the Second World War. Physician Druin Burch confirms this in his book *Taking the Medicine*. A few cherries – antibiotics, for instance – distract us, and so, drug researchers are celebrated while anti-smoking activists are not.

Administrative departments in large companies glorify themselves like hoteliers do. They are masters at showcasing all they have done, but they never communicate what they haven't achieved for the company. What should you do? If you sit on the supervisory board of such an organisation, ask about the 'leftover cherries', the failed projects and missed goals. You learn a lot more from this than from the successes. It is amazing how seldom such questions are asked. Second: instead of employing a horde of financial controllers to calculate costs to the nearest cent, double-check targets. You will be amazed to find that, over time, the original goals have faded. These have been replaced, quietly and secretly, with self-set goals that are always attainable. If you hear of such targets, alarm bells should sound. It is the equivalent of shooting an arrow and drawing a bull's-eye around where it lands.

See also **Story Bias** (ch. 13); **Self-Serving Bias** (ch. 45)

97

THE STONE-AGE HUNT
FOR SCAPEGOATS

Fallacy of the Single Cause

Chris Matthews is one of MSNBC's top journalists. In his news show, so-called political experts are wheeled on one after the other and interviewed. I've never understood what a political expert is, or why such a career is worthwhile. In 2003, the U.S. invasion of Iraq was the issue on everybody's lips. More important than the experts' answers were Chris Matthews' questions: 'What is *the motive* behind the war?' 'I wanted to know whether 9/11 is *the reason*, because a lot of people think it's payback?' 'Do you think that the weapons of mass destruction were *the reason* for this war?' 'Why do you think we invaded Iraq? The *real reason*, not the sales pitch?' And so on.

I can't abide questions like that any more. They are symptomatic of the most common of all mental errors, a mistake for which, strangely enough, there is no everyday term. For now, the awkward phrase, the *fallacy of the single cause*, will have to do.

Five years later, in 2008, panic reigned in the financial markets. Banks caved in and had to be nursed back to health with tax dollars. Investors, politicians and journalists probed furiously for the root of the crisis: Greenspan's loose monetary policy? The stupidity of investors? The dubious rating agencies? Corrupt auditors? Bad risk models? Pure greed? Not a single one, and yet every one of these, is the cause.

A balmy Indian summer, a friend's divorce, the First World War, cancer, a school shooting, the worldwide success of a company, the invention of writing – any clear-thinking person knows that no single factor leads to such events. Rather, there are hundreds, thousands, an infinite number of factors that add up. Still, we keep trying to pin the blame on just one.

'When an apple ripens and falls – what makes it fall? Is it that it is attracted to the ground, is it that the stem withers, is it that the sun has dried it up, that is has grown heavier, that the wind shakes it, that the boy standing underneath it wants to eat it? No one thing is the cause.' In this passage from *War and Peace*, Tolstoy hit the nail on the head.

Suppose you are the product manager for a well-known breakfast cereal brand. You have just launched an organic, low-sugar variety. After a month, it's painfully clear that the new product is a flop. How do you go about investigating the cause? First, you know that there will never be one sole factor. Take a sheet of paper and sketch out all the potential reasons. Do the same for the reasons behind these reasons. After a while, you will have a network of possible influencing factors. Second, highlight those you can change and delete those you cannot (such as 'human nature'). Third, conduct empirical tests by varying the highlighted factors in different markets. This costs time and money, but it's the only way to escape the swamp of superficial assumptions.

The *fallacy of the single cause* is as ancient as it is dangerous. We have learned to see people as the 'masters of their own destinies'. Aristotle proclaimed this 2,500 years ago. Today we know that it is wrong. The notion of free will is up for debate. Our actions are brought about by the interaction of thousands of factors – from genetic predisposition to upbringing, from education to the concentration of hormones between individual brain cells. Still we hold firmly to the old image of self-governance. This is not only wrong but also morally questionable. As long as we believe in singular reasons, we will always be able to trace triumphs or disasters back to individuals and stamp them 'responsible'. The idiotic hunt for a scapegoat goes hand-in-hand with the exercise of power – a game that people have been playing for thousands of years.

And yet, the *fallacy of the single cause* is so popular that Tracy Chapman was able to build her worldwide success on it. 'Give Me One Reason' is the song that secured her success. But hold on – weren't there a few others, too?

See also **'Because' Justification** (ch. 52); **Falsification of History** (ch. 78); **Hindsight Bias** (ch. 14); **Fundamental Attribution Error** (ch. 36)

98

SPEED DEMONS MAKE SAFE DRIVERS

Intention-To-Treat Error

You'll find it hard to believe, but speed demons drive more safely than so-called 'careful' drivers. Why? Well, consider this: the distance from Miami to West Palm Beach is around 75 miles. Drivers who cover the distance in an hour or less we'll categorise as 'reckless drivers' because they're travelling at an average of 75 mph or more. All others we put into the group of careful drivers. Which group experiences fewer accidents? Without a doubt, it is the 'reckless drivers'. They all completed the journey in less than an hour, so could not have been involved in any accidents. This automatically puts all drivers who end up in accidents in the slower drivers' category. This example illustrates a treacherous fallacy, the so-called *intention-to-treat error*. Unfortunately, there is no catchier term for it.

This might sound to you like the *survivorship bias* (chapter 1), but it's different. In the *survivorship bias* you only see the survivors, not the failed projects or cars involved in accidents. In the *intention-to-treat error*, the failed projects or cars with accidents show up prominently, just in the wrong category.

A banker showed me an interesting study recently. Its conclusion: companies with debt on their balance sheets are significantly more profitable than firms with no debt (equity only). The banker vehemently insisted that every company should borrow at will, and, of course, his bank is the best place to do it. I examined the study more closely. How could that be? Indeed, from 1,000 randomly selected firms, those with large loans displayed higher returns not only on their equity but also on their total capital. They were in every respect more successful than the independently financed firms. Then the penny dropped: unprofitable companies don't get corporate loans. Thus, they form part of the 'equity-only' group. The firms that make up this set have bigger cash cushions, stay afloat longer and, no matter how sickly they are, remain part of the study. On the other side, firms that have borrowed a lot go bankrupt more quickly. Once they cannot pay back the interest, the bank takes over, and the companies are sold off – thus disappearing from the sample. The ones that remain in the 'debt group' are relatively healthy, regardless of how much debt they have amassed on their balance sheets.

If you're thinking, 'OK, got it', watch out. The *intention-to-treat error* is not easy to recognise. A fictional example from medicine: a pharmaceutical company has developed a new drug to fight heart disease. A study 'proves' that it significantly reduces patients' mortality rates. The data speaks for itself: among patients who have taken the drug regularly, the five-year mortality rate is 15%. For those who have swallowed placebo pills, it is about the same, indicating that the pill doesn't work. However – and this is crucial – the mortality rate of patients who have taken the drug at irregular intervals is 30% – twice as high! A big difference between regular and irregular intake. So, the pill is a complete success. Or is it?

Here's the snag: the pill is probably not the decisive factor; rather, it is the patients' behaviour. Perhaps patients discontinued the pill following severe side effects and so landed in the 'irregular intake' category. Maybe they were so ill that there was no way to continue it on a regular basis. Either way, only relatively healthy patients remain in the 'regular' group, which makes the drug look a lot more effective than it really is. The really sick patients who, for this very reason, couldn't take the drug on a regular basis, ended up populating the 'irregular intake' group.

In reputable studies, medical researchers evaluate the data of all patients whom they originally intend to treat (hence the title); it doesn't matter if they take part in the trial or drop out. Unfortunately, many studies flout this rule. Whether this is intentional or accidental remains to be seen. Therefore, be on your guard: always check whether test subjects – drivers who end up in accidents, bankrupt companies, critically ill patients – have, for whatever reason, vanished from the sample. If so, you should file the study where it belongs: in the trashcan.

See also **Survivorship Bias** (ch. 1); **Will Rogers Phenomenon** (ch. 58)

99

WHY YOU SHOULDN'T READ THE NEWS

News Illusion

Earthquake in Sumatra. Plane crash in Russia. Man holds daughter captive in cellar for thirty years. Heidi Klum separates from Seal. Record salaries at Bank of America. Attack in Pakistan. Resignation of Mali's president. New world record in shot-put.

Do you really need to know all these things?

We are incredibly well informed yet we know incredibly little. Why? Because two centuries ago, we invented a toxic form of knowledge called 'news'. News is to the mind what sugar is to the body: appetising, easy to digest – and highly destructive in the long run.

Three years ago, I began an experiment. I stopped reading and listening to the news. I cancelled all newspaper and magazine subscriptions. Television and radio were disposed of. I deleted the news apps from my iPhone. I didn't touch a single free newspaper and deliberately looked the other way when someone on a plane tried to offer me any such reading material. The first weeks were hard. Very hard. I was constantly afraid of missing something. But after a while, I had a new outlook. The result after three years: clearer thoughts, more valuable insights, better decisions, and much more time. And the best thing? I haven't missed anything important. My social network – not Facebook, the one that exists in the real world consisting of flesh-and-blood friends and acquaintances – works as a news filter and keeps me in the loop.

A dozen reasons exist to give news a wide berth. Here are the top three. First, our brains react disproportionately to different types of information. Scandalous, shocking, people-based, loud, fast-changing details all stimulate us, whereas abstract, complex and unprocessed information sedates us. News producers capitalise on this. Gripping stories, garish images and sensational 'facts' capture our attention. Recall for a moment their business models: advertisers buy space and thus finance the news circus on the condition that their ads will be seen. The result: everything subtle, complex, abstract and profound must be systematically filtered out, even though such stories are much more relevant to our lives and to our understanding of the world. As a result of news consumption, we walk around with a distorted mental map of the risks and threats we actually face.

Second, news is irrelevant. In the past twelve months, you have probably consumed about 10,000 news snippets – perhaps as many as thirty per day. Be very honest: name one of them, just one, that helped you make a better decision – for your life, your career or your business – compared with not having this piece of news. No one I have asked has been able to name more than two useful news stories – out of 10,000. A miserable result. News organisations assert that their information gives you a competitive advantage. Too many fall for this. In reality, news consumption represents a competitive disadvantage. If news really helped people advance, journalists would be at the top of the income pyramid. They aren't – quite the opposite.

Third, news is a waste of time. An average human being squanders half a day each week on reading about current affairs. In global terms, this is an immense loss of productivity. Take the 2008 terror attacks in Mumbai. Out of sheer thirst for recognition, terrorists murdered 200 people. Let's say a billion people devoted an hour of their time to following the aftermath: they viewed the minute-by-minute updates and listened to the inane chatter of a few 'experts' and 'commentators'. This is a very realistic 'guesstimate' since India has more than a billion inhabitants. Thus our conservative calculation: one billion people multiplied by an hour's distraction equals one billion hours of work stoppage. If we convert this, we learn that news consumption wasted around 2,000 lives – ten times more than the attack. A sarcastic but accurate observation.

I would predict that turning your back on news will benefit you as much as purging any of the other ninety-eight flaws we have covered in the pages of this book. Kick the habit – completely. Instead, read long background articles and books. Yes, nothing beats books for understanding the world.

See also **Fundamental Attribution Error** (ch. 36); **Sleeper Effect** (ch. 70); **Confirmation Bias** (ch. 7–8); **Information Bias** (ch. 59); **Personification** (ch. 87); **Story Bias** (ch. 13)

EPILOGUE

The Pope asked Michelangelo: 'Tell me the secret of your genius. How have you created the statue of David, the masterpiece of all masterpieces?' Michelangelo's answer: 'It's simple. I removed everything that is not David.'

Let's be honest. We don't know for sure what makes us successful. We can't pinpoint exactly what makes us happy. But we know with certainty what destroys success or happiness. This realisation, as simple as it is, is fundamental: Negative knowledge (what *not* to do) is much more potent than positive knowledge (what to do).

Thinking more clearly and acting more shrewdly means adopting Michelangelo's method: don't focus on David. Instead, focus on everything that is not David and chisel it away. In our case: eliminate all errors and better thinking will follow.

The Greeks, Romans and medieval thinkers had a term for this approach: *via negativa*. Literally the negative path, the path of renunciation, of exclusion, of reduction. Theologians were the first to tread the *via negativa*: we cannot say what God is; we can only say what God is not. Applied to the present day: we cannot say what brings us success. We can pin down only what blocks or obliterates success. Eliminate the downside, the thinking errors, and the upside will take care of itself. This is all we need to know.

As a novelist and company founder, I have fallen into a variety of traps. Fortunately I was always able to free myself from them. Nowadays when I hold presentations in front of doctors, CEOs, board members, investors, politicians or government officials, I sense a kinship. I feel that we are sitting in the same boat – after all, we are all trying to row through life without getting swallowed up by the maelstroms. Still, many people are uneasy with the *via negativa*. It is counter-intuitive. It is even countercultural, flying in the face of contemporary wisdom. But look around and you'll find plenty of examples of the *via negativa* at work. This is what the legendary investor Warren Buffett writes about himself and his partner Charlie Munger: 'Charlie and I have not learned how to solve difficult business problems. What we have learned is to avoid them.' Welcome to the *via negativa*.

I have listed almost 100 thinking errors in this book without answering the question: what are thinking errors anyway? What is irrationality? Why do we fall into these traps? Two theories of irrationality exist: a *hot* and a *cold*. The *hot* theory is as old as the hills. Here is Plato's analogy: a rider steers wildly galloping horses; the rider signifies reason and the galloping horses embody emotions. Reason tames feelings. If this fails, irrationality runs free. Another example: feelings are like bubbling lava. Usually, reason can keep a lid on them, but every now and then the lava of irrationality erupts. Hence *hot* irrationality. There is no reason to fret about logic: it is error-free; it's just that, sometimes, emotions overpower it.

This hot theory of irrationality boiled and bubbled for centuries. For John Calvin, the founder of a strict form of

Protestantism in the 1500s, such feelings represented evil, and only by focusing on God could you repel them. People who underwent volcanic eruptions of emotion were of the devil. They were tortured and killed. According to Austrian psychoanalyst Sigmund Freud's theory, the rationalist 'ego' and the moralistic 'superego' control the impulsive 'id'. But that theory holds less water in the real world. Forget about obligation and discipline. To believe that we can completely control our emotions through thinking is illusory – as illusory as trying to make your hair grow by willing it to.

On the other hand, the *cold* theory of irrationality is still young. After the Second World War, many searched for explanations about the irrationality of the Nazis. Emotional outbursts were rare in Hitler's leadership ranks. Even his fiery speeches were nothing more than masterful performances. It was not molten eruptions but stone-cold calculation that resulted in the Nazi madness. The same can be said of Stalin or of the Khmer Rouge.

In the 1960s, psychologists began to do away with Freud's claims and to examine our thinking, decisions, and actions scientifically. The result was a cold theory of irrationality that states: thinking is in itself not pure, but prone to error. This affects everyone. Even highly intelligent people fall into the same cognitive traps. Likewise, errors are not randomly distributed. We systematically err in the same direction. That makes our mistakes predictable, and thus fixable to a degree – but only to a degree, never completely. For a few decades, the origins of these errors remained in the dark. Everything else in our body is relatively reliable – heart, muscles, lungs, immune system. Why should our brains of all things experience lapse after lapse?

Thinking is a biological phenomenon. Evolution has shaped it just as it has the forms of animals or the colours of flowers. Suppose we could go back 50,000 years, grab hold of an ancestor and bring him back with us into the present. We send him to the hairdresser and put him in a Hugo Boss suit. Would he stand out on the street? No. Of course, he would have to learn English, how to drive and how to operate a cellphone, but we had to learn those things, too. Biology has dispelled all doubt: physically, and that includes cognitively, we are hunter-gatherers in Hugo Boss (or H&M, as the case may be).

What has changed markedly since ancient times is the environment in which we live. Back then, things were simple and stable. We lived in small groups of about fifty people. There was no significant technological or social progress. Only in the last 10,000 years did the world begin to transform dramatically, with the development of crops, livestock, villages, cities, global trade and financial markets. Since industrialisation, little is left of the environment for which our brain is optimised. If you spend fifteen minutes in a shopping mall, you will pass more people than our ancestors saw during their entire lifetimes. Whoever claims to know how the world will look in ten years is made into a laughing stock less than a year after such a pronouncement. In the past 10,000 years, we have created a world that we no longer understand. Everything is more sophisticated, but also more complex and interdependent. The result is overwhelming material prosperity, but also lifestyle diseases (such as type two diabetes, lung cancer and depression) and errors in thinking. If the complexity continues to rise – and it will, that much is certain – these errors will only increase and intensify.

In our hunter-gatherer past, activity paid off more often than reflection did. Lightning-fast reactions were vital and long ruminations were ruinous. If your hunter-gatherer buddies suddenly bolted, it made sense to follow suit – regardless of whether a sabre-tooth tiger or a boar had startled them. If you failed to run away, and it turned out to be a tiger, the price of a first-degree error was death. On the other hand, if you had just fled from a boar, this lesser mistake would have only cost you a few calories. It paid to be wrong about the same things. Whoever was wired differently exited the gene pool after the first or second incidence. We are the descendants of those *homines sapientes* who tend to scarper when the crowd does. But in the modern world, this intuitive behaviour is disadvantageous. Today's world rewards single-minded contemplation and independent action. Anyone who has fallen victim to stock market hype has witnessed that.

Evolutionary psychology is still mostly a theory, but a very convincing one. It explains the majority of flaws, though not all of them. Consider the following statement: 'Every Hershey bar comes in a brown wrapper. Thus, every candy bar in a brown wrapper must be a Hershey bar.' Even intelligent people are susceptible to this flawed conclusion – so are native tribes that, for the most part, remain untouched by civilisation. Our hunter-gatherer ancestors were certainly not impervious to faulty logic. Some bugs in our thinking are hard-wired and have nothing to do with the 'mutation' of our environment.

Why is that? Evolution does not 'optimise' us completely. As long as we advance beyond our competitors (i.e., beat the Neanderthals), we can get away with error-laced behaviour. Consider the cuckoo. For hundreds of thousands of years, they have laid their eggs in the nests of songbirds, which then incubate and even feed the cuckoo chicks. This represents a behavioural error that evolution has not erased from the smaller birds; it is not deemed to be serious enough.

A second, parallel explanation of why our mistakes are so persistent took shape in the late 1990s. Our brains are designed to reproduce rather than search for the truth. In other words, we use our thoughts primarily to persuade. Whoever convinces others secures power and thus access to resources. Such assets represent a major advantage for mating and for rearing offspring. That truth is, at best, a secondary focus is reflected in the book market: novels sell much better than non-fiction titles, in spite of the latter's superior candour.

Finally, a third explanation exists. Intuitive decisions, even if they lack logic, are better under certain circumstances. So-called heuristic research deals with this topic. For many decisions, we lack the necessary information, so we are forced to use mental shortcuts and rules of thumb (heuristics). If you are drawn to different potential romantic partners, you must evaluate whom to marry. This is not a rational decision; if you rely solely on logic, you will remain single forever. In short, we often decide intuitively and justify our choices later. Many decisions (career, life partner, investments) take place subconsciously. A fraction of a second later, we construct a reason so that we feel we made a conscious choice. Alas, we do not behave like scientists, who are purely interested in objective facts. Instead, we think like lawyers, crafting the best possible justification for a predetermined conclusion.

So, forget about the 'left and right brain' that semi-intelligent self-help books describe. Much more important is the difference between intuitive and rational thinking. Both have legitimate applications. The intuitive mind is swift, spontaneous, and energy-saving. Rational thinking is slow, demanding, and energy-guzzling (in the form of blood sugar). Nobody has described this better than the great Daniel Kahneman in *Thinking, Fast and Slow*.

Since I started to collect cognitive errors, people often ask me how I manage to live an error-free life. The answer is: I don't. In fact, I don't even try. Just like everybody else I make snap decisions by consulting not my thoughts, but my feelings. For the most part I substitute the question, 'What do I think about this?' with 'How do I feel about this?' Quite frankly, anticipating and avoiding fallacies is a costly undertaking.

To make things simple, I have set myself the following rules: in situations where the possible consequences are large (i.e. important personal or business decisions), I try to be as reasonable and rational as possible when choosing. I take out my list of errors, and check them off one by one, just like a pilot does. I've created a handy checklist decision tree, and I use it to examine important decisions with a fine-tooth comb. In situations where the consequences are small (i.e. regular or diet Pepsi, sparkling or flat water?) I forget about rational optimisation and let my intuition take over. Thinking is tiring. Therefore, if the potential harm is small, don't rack your brains; such errors won't do lasting damage. You'll live better like this. Nature doesn't seem to mind if our decisions are perfect or not, as long as we can manoeuvre ourselves through life – and as long as we are ready to be rational when it comes to the crunch. And there's one other area where I let my intuition take the lead: when I am in my *circle of competence*. If you practise an instrument, you learn the notes and tell your fingers how to play them. Over time, you know the keys or the strings inside out. You see a musical score and your hands play the notes almost automatically. Warren Buffett reads balance sheets like professional musicians read scores. This is his *circle of competence*, the field he intuitively understands and masters. So, find out where your circle of competence is. Get a clear grasp of it. Hint: it's smaller than you think. If you face a consequential decision outside that circle, apply the hard, slow, rational thinking. For everything else, give your intuition free rein.

ACKNOWLEDGMENTS

Thanks to Nassim Nicholas Taleb for inspiring me to write this book, even if his advice was not to publish it under any circumstances. Alas, he encouraged me to write novels, arguing that non-fiction isn't 'sexy'. Thanks to Koni Gebistorf, who masterfully edited the original German texts, and to Nicky Griffin who translated the book to English (when she was away from her office at Google). I couldn't have picked better publishers and editors than Hollis Heimbouch from HarperCollins and Drummond Moir from Sceptre who has given these chapters their final finesse. Thanks to the scientists of the ZURICH.MINDS community for the countless debates about the state of research. Special thanks go to Gerd Gigerenzer, Roy Baumeister, Leda Cosmides, John Tooby, Robert Cialdini, Jonathan Haidt, Ernst Fehr, Bruno Frey, Iris Bohnet, Dan Golstein, Tomáš Sedláček and the philosopher John Gray for the enlightening conversations. I also thank my literary agent, John Brockman and his superb crew, for helping me with both the American and British editions of this book. Thanks to Frank Schirrmacher for finding space for my columns in the *Frankfurter Allgemeine Zeitung*, to Giovanni di Lorenzo and Moritz Mueller-Wirth for their publication in *Die Zeit* (Germany), and to Martin Spieler who gave them a good home in Switzerland's *Sonntagszeitung*. Without the weekly pressure to forge one's thoughts into a readable format, my notes would never have been published in book form.

For everything that appears here after the countless stages of editing, I alone bear the responsibility. My greatest thanks go to my wife, Sabine Ried, who proves to me every day that the 'good life' – as defined by Aristotle – consists of far more than clear thoughts and clever actions.

Rolf Dobelli, born 1966, is a Swiss writer, novelist and entrepreneur. He has an MBA and a PhD in economic philosophy from the University of St. Gallen, Switzerland. Dobelli is co-founder of getAbstract, the world's leading provider of book summaries. Most famously, he is author of THE ART OF THINKING CLEARLY, which became an instant success and landed on the number 1 spot on Germany's official bestseller list and has been translated into many languages. Dobelli is also founder and curator of ZURICH.MINDS, an invitation-only community of the most distinguished thinkers, scientists and artists.

www.rolfdobelli.com

www.facebook.com/dobelli

A NOTE ON SOURCES

Hundreds of studies have been conducted on the vast majority of cognitive and behavioural errors. The knowledge encompassed in this book is based on the research carried out in the fields of cognitive and social psychology over the past three decades. For full references, as well as recommendations for further reading and comments, visit www.sceptrebooks.co.uk/AOTC.

INDEX